D1142288

MARY GWYNN'S
30-MINUTE VEGETARIAN

MARY GWYNN'S
30-MINUTE
VEGETARIAN

MEREHURST

To my husband, Mark

Published in 1995 by Merehurst Limited
Ferry House, 51-57 Lacy Road, Putney, London SW15 1PR

Copyright © 1995 Mary Gwynn

ISBN 1-85391-400-2

A catalogue record for this book is available from the
British Library.

Editor: Beverly Le Blanc
Design: Hammond Hammond
Photographer: Ken Field
Home economist: Louise Pickford
Home economist's assistant: Carol Tennant
Stylist: Suzy Gittins
Typesetter: Michael Weintroub

Colour separation by Global Colour, Malaysia
Printed in Singapore by CS Graphics Pte Ltd

NOTES

A standard spoon measurement is used in all recipes:

1 teaspoon = one 5 ml spoon
1 tablespoon = one 15 ml spoon
All spoon measures are rounded.

All eggs are size 3 unless otherwise specified.

Ovens should be preheated to the specified temperature.

For all recipes, quantities are given metric and imperial. Follow one set
of measures but not a mixture as they are not interchangeable.

Frontispiece: Mixed Pepper and Mozzarella Bruschetta, see page 18

FOREWORD

Fast food has become an essential in today's busy lives but I really believe that there is no reason why quality and flavour should suffer because of a lack of time. This book represents a slow distillation of the way I have cooked over the past ten years – what has emerged is simple food made from fresh ingredients (and I have to admit, normally prepared in a hurry), enjoyed at leisure by family and friends. So many different people have influenced this personal style; one of the main pleasures I have found from working with food has been that you learn something from everyone you meet or work alongside. Ideas are taken up, adapted and juggled with, to re-emerge with your own slant. I hope that is exactly what you will do with these recipes. Try them and then develop them to suit your own tastes.

Most of the recipes fit easily into 30 minutes preparation and cooking time; I certainly don't have more time or inclination in the evening. A couple may just slip over the half hour mark but need little supervision so you are not standing over them as they cook. All are ideally suited for mid-week meals when a single dish served with good bread and a salad is all you need, but they can just as easily be put together to create a most satisfying dinner for friends.

You will find the ingredients are straight forward with a few little luxuries thrown in – a selection of basic staples that are always in the storecupboard and re-stocked at the weekly shop, supplemented with whatever is the freshest and most tempting spotted on my journey home.

For me, cooking without meat has led to a re-discovery of the joys of seasonal veg and fruit – the flavours, colours and tastes highlighted as these ingredients take centre stage in each meal.

You will find that most of the recipes serve two and a few just one. I know very few people who ever cook for four regularly, and this book reflects that. Also I think it's usually easier to double up on a recipe than it is to divide it in half. Pasta and rice dishes follow Italian serving portions with at least 90 g (3 oz) dry weight per head.

I have never been a fan of ready-prepared spice mixes and usually keep a stock of individual spices and mix my own as I need them. However, in recent years the range available has increased so much as we all cook so many exotic dishes on a regular basis, that my cupboard is often overflowing with jars past their use-by date. So with the added spurs of lack of time and a great improvement in the quality of what's around, I do use jars of spice pastes for mid-week cooking. Buy the best available – there will be a huge difference in the final result.

Mary Gwynn

Introduction

page 8

Soups and snacks

page 10

Lentils
and other pulses

page 22

Pasta dishes

page 34

Vegetable dishes and salads

Rice and grain dishes

Egg and cheese dishes

Desserts

INTRODUCTION

A desire for better health has been recognised as one of the major triggers for turning people to a vegetarian diet. However, cutting out meat, be it altogether or just part of the time, will not automatically ensure good health. Recent research that has pinpointed markedly lower rates of cancer and heart disease amongst vegetarians does not lay all the blame at meat's door. What seems to be behind the figures is that the vegetarian diet is more likely to be high in fresh vegetables and fruit, fibre and starch and low in saturated fat, all of which puts it into the dietary guidelines set out by the World Health Organisation.

Most of the recipes here are based on these recommendations, so use them within the following framework: aim to eat at least five portions of fresh fruit and vegetables a day; starches, such as bread, pasta or rice, with every meal; and remember that fat should only make up thirty percent of your daily intake, so try to avoid the common mistake of replacing meat with high-fat dairy products. The Italians have it about right when they serve large bowls of pasta flavoured with small amounts of a flavourful sauce.

INGREDIENTS GUIDE

I have used readily available ingredients for the recipes in this book as I realise that few people have the time or energy to search out unusual foods unless it's for a special occasion. I do, however, keep a selection of so-called luxury ingredients to hand to add a little interest here and there when I'm cooking in a hurry. Some of them may, at first glance, seem extravagant but on the whole they are added to dishes in proportions that are modest to their final impact on the finished dish. You can substitute other ingredients and I have indicated where this will work but I think that

to enjoy vegetarian cooking (in fact, any style of cooking!) to its full scope and range, top-quality basic ingredients are the key.

CHEESES

If you are new to a meat-free diet or are using this book to cook for a vegetarian guest, I want to point out that many cheeses are not suitable for inclusion in a vegetarian diet as they are made with the animal by-product, rennet, which is added during the cheese-making process to coagulate the milk. However, there are increasing numbers of cheeses available made with an alternative.

Most block Parmesan cheese is not suitable but there is a ready-grated one from Italy in some supermarkets, and the makers intend to make it available in block form soon. In fact, it may be in the shops by the time this book is out. As I don't follow a strict vegetarian diet, I always use freshly grated as the flavour bears no relation to the dry dust of the ready prepared one, and though it is expensive you only need a little. Store the block wrapped in foil in the cheese drawer of your fridge.

OILS

I keep several types of oil in the cupboard; sunflower or rapeseed oil and a supermarket extra virgin olive oil for every day use, and small bottles of walnut and sesame oil for use as flavourings. I have to admit that I use extra virgin oil for everything except Indian or oriental cooking, where the flavour would be too strong. This may seem extravagant but as we save by not eating meat and basing meals on cheap pulses, pasta and rice, I can justify it to myself, and the flavour and health benefits more than balance the cost. I also keep a bottle of estate-bottled extra virgin oil to hand for drizzling on soups, salads and pasta as a final seasoning. This is expensive – but I use it very sparingly, and only treat myself to the occasional bottle or ask for one as a present!

BREAD AND BUTTER

There is now a move back to butter as the hydrogenating process used to solidify vegetable and animal fat to make margarine gets the thumbs down from the health experts. I never made the change in the first place – as with many cooks, butter's superior flavour and versatility for cooking has ensured its place in my kitchen. Still, moderation is the key, so I cook with olive oil and use a little butter to spread on my toast first thing in the morning, for the odd sauce and for baking when it's flavour is unbeatable.

Try to get used to eating bread without butter if you can; this is easy as so many interesting new speciality breads are available. I keep a couple of loaves of my favourites, such as olive ciabatta, French walnut and various naan breads, handy in the freezer and heat them from frozen.

VINEGARS

Balsamic vinegar is aged in wooden casks like a fine wine which gives it an intense caramel aroma and distinctive sweet-sour taste. It is useful for adding an extra depth of flavour to dressings, casseroles and sauces. I use a super-market version but the more expensive ones available from delicatessens and specialist shops are far superior, so I recommend that you treat yourself to a bottle. Red wine vinegar can be substituted in most recipes.

DRIED VEGETABLES

Sun-dried tomatoes, like balsamic vinegar, have been hailed as the trendy new ingredient of the 90s, and like many fashions, when the fuss dies down they may get relegated to the back of the cupboard. It would, however, be a pity if this is be the case with such a versatile ingredient. Add them to soups, pasta sauces and cheese dishes for a wonderfully intense tomato flavour. They are available either dried or in oil – the dried version needs to be soaked in hot water for 15 minutes before use, and don't waste the soaking liquid because it makes excellent stock. Stored in oil, the reconstituted tomatoes can be sliced and used straight from the jar, ideal for salads and sandwiches. Use the oil in dressings and also for frying.

Dried mushrooms come in different varieties – the range of oddities available in Chinese supermarkets definitely need insider knowledge, but ceps, or porcini, as they are known in Italy, are a real boon for meat-free cooking. Reconstituted in the same way as the tomatoes, they have a marvellous rich, earthy flavour that adds a much-needed boost to stocks and heartier dishes.

Luckily a little goes a very long way, as dried mushrooms seem on first acquaintance to be prohibitively expensive but you rarely need more than 7 g (¼ oz) for a dish for four, so do not be put off by the cost.

HERBS

I keep fresh basil growing all year round on my windowsill and grow most of the other herbs I use regularly, such as rosemary, thyme, tarragon and chives, in pots on the patio. I've never been very successful with parsley, so I buy it weekly, and always choose the flat-leaf version, which I consider to have a far superior flavour. If you don't have ready access to fresh herbs, choose the freeze dried ones – they aren't a patch on fresh but are a great improvement on normal dried. Dill and tarragon are well worth keeping in stock.

Soups and snacks

Quick suppers are what this book is all about, basically one-course meals with something simple to finish. Soups fit perfectly into this category. There are also times when I want to serve a simple starter, or just fancy something on a tray. The recipes in this chapter are for these occasions.

SUMMER VEGETABLE SOUP WITH PESTO

Time to make: about 5 minutes
Time to cook: 25 minutes

Serves 2

½ **small onion**

½ **stick celery**

½ **garlic clove**

1 **tomato**

½ **small carrot**

1 **small potato**

60 g (2 oz) **Savoy cabbage**

60 g (2 oz) **green beans**

60 g (2 oz) **broccoli**

1 tablespoon **olive oil**

625 ml (20 fl oz) **vegetable stock**

30 g (1 oz) **macaroni**

1½ tablespoons **pesto sauce**

salt and freshly ground black pepper

freshly grated Parmesean cheese, to serve

Really expensive, first pressed extra virgin olive oil should be used sparingly, like a seasoning, rather than for frying or in mayonnaise. I find that a dash of my favourite extra virgin olive oil added just before serving really enhances the flavour of the pesto in this fresh-tasting soup. Warm olive bread is delicious with this.

1 To prepare the vegetables, chop the onion, celery, garlic and tomato. Peel and dice the carrot and potato. Shred the cabbage, then cut the green beans and broccoli into short lengths.
2 Heat the oil in a large saucepan over a medium heat. Add the onion, celery, carrot and garlic and cook, stirring occasionally, for 3 minutes until softened but not browned.
3 Stir in the cabbage, green beans and broccoli and continue cooking for a further 2 minutes.
4 Stir in the tomato, stock and salt and pepper. Bring to the boil, then lower the heat and simmer for 10 minutes until the vegetables are almost tender.
5 Stir in the pasta, increase the heat slightly and continue simmering for a further 10 minutes until the pasta is tender.
6 Stir in the pesto, then check the seasoning and serve with grated Parmesan cheese sprinkled over the top.

Cook's Tip
You can use any selection of vegetables for this soup. I tend to buy a selection at the weekend to use in dishes such as this, but what actually goes in each soup varies every time I make it.

Stirring in the pesto sauce.

CHILLI BEAN SOUP

Time to make: about 10 minutes
Time to cook: 20 minutes

Serves 2

1 small red onion

½ garlic clove

400 g (14 oz) can red kidney beans

1 tablespoon olive oil

½ teaspoon chilli powder

½ teaspoon ground cumin

1½ tablespoons tomato purée

½ tablespoon lemon juice

1 tablespoon vegetarian Worcestershire sauce

few drops Tabasco sauce

625 ml (20 fl oz) vegetable stock

salt and freshly ground black pepper

Topping

30 g (1 oz) vegetarian Cheddar cheese

4 slices French bread

This recipe first appeared in the pages of *Vegetarian Good Food* and it was so popular that I've included it here for those who missed it. It freezes well but the chilli flavour intensifies the longer you keep it, so use less chilli powder if you intend to make extra for your freezer.

1   To prepare the vegetables, chop the onion and crush the garlic. Drain and rinse the kidney beans.
2   Heat the oil in a large saucepan over a medium heat. Add the onion and garlic and cook for 3 minutes until softened but not browned.
3   Stir in the kidney beans, chilli powder, cumin, tomato purée, lemon juice, Worcestershire sauce, Tabasco sauce and stock. Bring to the boil, then lower the heat, cover and simmer for 15 minutes until the vegetables and beans are tender.
4   Meanwhile, grate the cheese for the topping. Preheat the grill to high.
5   Transfer all the ingredients to a blender or food processor and purée the soup until smooth, then return it to the cleaned pan. Re-heat it but do not allow it to boil.
6   Pour the hot soup into flameproof soup bowls. Float slices of French bread on top and sprinkle with the cheese. Place the bowls under the grill until the cheese melts, then serve.

Cook's Tip
If you think you will be rushed at mealtime, you can purée the soup up to 2 days ahead and keep it covered in the fridge. Then to serve, just re-heat it and grill the topping.

GREEN RICE SOUP

Time to make: about 5 minutes
Time to cook: 20 to 25 minutes

Serves 2

½ small onion

1 small turnip

1 small carrot

185 g (6 oz) spring greens

625 ml (20 fl oz) vegetable stock

1 tablespoon olive oil

4 or 5 strands saffron

45 g (1½ oz) risotto rice

salt and freshly ground black pepper

extra virgin olive oil and freshly grated Parmesan cheese, to serve

Both the Italians and Spanish have versions of this soup. Short-grain rice is grown in abundance in both countries, giving the national rice dishes their individual characteristics – Italian risottos and Spanish paellas both have creamy textures with a wonderful bite to the rice. I use risotto rice in this soup as more authentic Spanish rice is not so readily available, but you can also use a long-grain white rice and the cooking time will be reduced to 12 to 15 minutes.

1 To prepare the vegetables, finely chop the onion and peel and dice the turnip and carrot. Remove any tough cores from the spring greens, then shred them.
2 In a small saucepan, over a medium heat, heat the stock until it is simmering.
3 Meanwhile, heat the oil in a large saucepan over a medium heat. Add the onion and cook, stirring occasionally, for 3 minutes until softened but not browned. Stir in the turnip, carrot and spring greens and continue simmering until the greens wilt.
4 Mix the saffron with 1½ tablespoons of the simmering stock in a small heatproof bowl, then add it to the pan along with the remaining stock and salt and pepper.
5 Bring the mixture to the boil, then stir in the rice, lower the heat and simmer for 15 to 20 minutes until the rice is tender. Check the seasoning and serve with extra virgin olive oil and freshly grated Parmesan sprinkled over the top.

Cook's Tip
Swiss chard is an excellent substitute for the spring greens in this soup if you can find it or grow your own.

GRILLED TOMATO SOUP WITH TARRAGON

Time to make: 10 minutes
Time to cook: 10 minutes

Serves 2

2 large beef tomatoes, about 500 g (1 lb)

6 spring onions

1 large slice white bread

1 or 2 garlic cloves

1 teaspoon tomato purée

2 tablespoons chopped fresh tarragon

1 teaspoon red wine vinegar

315 ml (10 fl oz) tomato juice

155 ml (5 fl oz) iced water

1 tablespoon extra virgin olive oil

salt and freshly ground black pepper

tarragon leaves and diced cucumber, to garnish

When the weather starts to get warm my husband starts asking for gazpacho, the wonderfully refreshing Spanish chilled tomato soup.

This is an emergency version created when the only salad vegetables I had in the fridge were tomatoes. Grilling or roasting tomatoes really brings out the full flavour that may otherwise be lacking in many of the shop-bought specimens. I usually make this cold soup with beef tomatoes but substitute Italian plum tomatoes when I can get them.

1 Preheat the grill to high. To prepare the vegetables, halve the tomatoes and chop the spring onions.
2 Arrange the tomatoes, skin sides down, on the grill pan and grill for about 10 minutes, turning them over after 5 minutes, until the skins are blackened all over and all the flesh is soft.
3 Meanwhile, cut the crusts off the bread and crush the garlic cloves.
4 Scoop the tomato flesh into a blender or food processor. Add the bread, garlic, tomato purée, tarragon, vinegar, tomato juice, water and olive oil and process until smooth. Check the seasoning and chill until ready to serve.
5 To serve, garnish with tarragon leaves and diced cucumber and serve with crusty bread.

Cook's Tip
To chill this soup quickly, serve it with a couple of ice cubes floating on top.

Grilled Tomato Soup with Tarragon served with Grilled Aubergine on Olive Bread with Tomato Salsa, see page 20.

WINTER VEGETABLE BROTH

Time to make: 5 minutes
Time to cook: 25 to 50 minutes

Serves 2

1 small onion
1 small carrot
1 small turnip
½ small swede
½ leek
½ tablespoon olive oil
30 g (1 oz) pearl barley
625 ml (20 fl oz) vegetable stock
salt and freshly ground black pepper
chopped fresh parsley, to garnish

Pearl barley gives flavour and texture to this simple soup, but adding it does push the cooking time over the 30-minute mark. However, I've included the barley because it adds valuable protein to the dish, but leave it out if you haven't got the time. Instead, just cook the vegetables for 20 minutes and serve this soup with wholemeal bread and cheese for a balanced meal.

1 To prepare the vegetables, chop the onion, finely cube the carrot, turnip and swede and slice the leek.
2 Heat the oil in a large pan, then add the onion, carrot, turnip, swede and leek and cook over a medium heat for 3 to 4 minutes without browning. Add the barley and continue cooking for 1 minute.
3 Stir in the stock and seasoning and bring to the boil, then lower the heat, cover and simmer for 45 minutes until the barley and vegetables are tender. Adjust the seasoning and serve in bowls sprinkled with parsley.

Cook's Tip
This recipe also makes a tasty smooth soup. Just omit the barley and purée the cooked vegetables and stock in a blender or food processor until smooth. Stir in 6 tablespoons single cream and serve sprinkled with chopped chives.

THICK LEEK AND LENTIL SOUP

Time to make: 5 minutes
Time to cook: 25 minutes

Serves 2

½ large onion

1½ stalks celery

1 carrot

1 large leek

1½ tablespoons olive oil

½ tablespoon tomato purée

90 g (3 oz) red lentils

625 ml (20 fl oz) vegetable stock

2 cloves

1 small bay leaf

½ teaspoon vegetarian Worcestershire sauce

salt and freshly ground black pepper

finely chopped fresh parsley, to garnish

Soup, bread and cheese make up a standard winter Saturday lunch in my house, and I often make double quantities of this soup and freeze it to use the extra for the kids' packed lunches. Red lentils make a tasty, filling soup – this really comes into its own on Bonfire night for instant internal central heating!

1   To prepare the vegetables, slice the onion, celery, carrot and leek.
2   Heat the oil in a large saucepan, add the onion, celery, carrot and leek and cook over a medium heat, stirring occasionally, until softened but not browned.
3   Stir in the tomato purée, lentils, stock, cloves, bay leaf, Worcestershire sauce and seasoning. Bring to the boil, then lower the heat and simmer, half covered, for about 20 minutes until the lentils are tender.
4   Transfer the soup to a blender or food processor and purée until smooth, then return to the rinsed-out pan. Re-heat the soup, but do not boil. Check the soup for seasoning, then serve in a large bowl with parsley scattered over the top.

Cook's Tip
Use any pulse in this soup instead of the lentils, as long as you use a canned variety so it doesn't need lengthy soaking and cooking. I have been very happy with the results when I have used canned borlotti beans and pale green haricot beans.

MIXED PEPPER AND MOZZARELLA BRUSCHETTA

Time to make: 5 to 10 minutes
Time to grill: about 10 minutes

Serves 2

½ **red pepper**

½ **yellow pepper**

1 small red onion

155 g (5 oz) mozzarella or goat's cheese

3 tablespoons olive oil

1 tablespoon chopped fresh oregano

2 large slices country-style bread

1 garlic clove, halved

salt and freshly ground black pepper

This is my version of open sandwichs with a distinctly Italian taste. I use whatever bread I have to hand: ciabatta, French walnut bread or even an English cottage loaf, though an open-crumbed bread soaks up the juices best. This recipe makes a luxurious but simple snack lunch, and my pepper-loving children adore it.

1   Preheat the grill to high. To prepare the vegetables, core and seed the red and yellow pepper halves. Cut the onion in half.
2   Under the hot grill, grill the peppers and onions on both sides until blackened all over. Place the peppers in a plastic bag for 2 minutes for the skins to soften, then skin and cut into strips. Slice the onions. Coarsely grate or crumble the cheese.
3   Put the pepper and onion slices in a bowl with half the olive oil, the oregano, cheese and seasoning.
4   Toast the bread on both sides under the grill, then rub one side of each slice with the cut garlic clove.
5   Drizzle with the remaining oil and top with the pepper mixture. Serve immediately.

Cook's Tips
I aways use my best extra-virgin olive oil for bruschetta as the flavour makes all the difference. In fact, you can serve the toasted bread simply rubbed with garlic and then drizzled with the oil for a delicious snack. To ring the changes for toppings, I sometimes add one shredded sun-dried tomato in oil to the mix, or 3 or 4 coarsely chopped black olives or capers, or a mixture of both.

Mixed Pepper and Mozzarella Bruschetta

GRILLED AUBERGINE ON OLIVE BREAD WITH TOMATO SALSA

Time to make: 5 to 10 minutes
Time to grill: 10 to 15 minutes

Serves 2

1 aubergine, about 250 g (8 oz)
½ garlic clove
2 tablespoons olive oil
1 tablespoon chopped fresh mint
salt and freshly ground black pepper
½ loaf ciabatta bread with black olives

Tomato Salsa

½ green chilli
1 plum tomato
1 spring onion

Photographed on page 15

This dish works well on the barbecue as the aubergine picks up a wonderful smoky flavour from the coals. But if you're not having a barbecue, don't worry because it is still good prepared under the grill, as the mint-flavoured oil gives its own kick.

1   Preheat the grill to high. To prepare the aubergine, cut it lengthways into slices about 0.5 cm (¼ in) thick. Chop the garlic.
2   Put the oil, garlic, mint and salt and pepper in a bowl and mix together.
3   Arrange the aubergine slices on the grill pan and brush with half the oil mixture. Grill for about 5 minutes until golden, then turn the slices over and brush the other side. Grill again until golden.
4   Meanwhile, make the tomato salsa. Seed the chilli. Put the chilli, the tomato, spring onion and salt and pepper in a blender or food processor and process until chopped; the salsa should be quite coarse, not a purée.
5   Split the bread in half horizontally, then each piece in half again. Toast on both sides under the grill.
6   Arrange the aubergine slices on top of the slices of toast. Serve with the tomato salsa.

Cook's Tip
I also use this method to make a quick aubergine and pepper salad – make up extra of the oil mixture and brush it over halved peppers, then grill them alongside the aubergine. Layer up in a serving dish and leave until the vegetables are at room temperature before serving.

SPICED CASHEWS AND ALMONDS

Time to make: 2 minutes
Time to cook: 5 minutes

Serves 2 to 4

1 large clove garlic

2 tablespoons sunflower oil

pinch of cayenne pepper

¼ teaspoon ground cumin

¼ teaspoon ground coriander

60 g (2 oz) unsalted cashews

60 g (2 oz) blanched almonds

coarse sea salt

I am never organised enough to make dainty little pre-dinner nibbles when we entertain, and I stopped buying large bags of American-style crisps when I realised it was all too easy to get through a bag all on my own before anyone else arrived! So now, friends usually get a packet of dry-roasted nuts if they are lucky, or a slice or two of toasted baguette spread with black olive paste. If they are very fortunate, however, I make these spicy nuts. I think these are ideal because I have the ingredients to hand and they are incredibly quick to prepare. They also go well as a side dish with a vegetable curry or the biryani on page 70.

1   Thinly slice the garlic, then cut it into slivers.
2   Heat the oil in a frying pan until almost smoking, then add the garlic, cayenne, cumin and coriander and stir for 30 seconds until the garlic is golden.
3   Add the nuts and stir over a medium heat for 3 to 4 minutes until they are golden brown. Take care not to let them burn.
4   Remove the nuts from the pan with a slotted spoon and drain well on kitchen paper. Sprinkle with sea salt and serve warm or at room temperature.

Cook's Tip
Use any selection of nuts for this recipe as long as they haven't been presalted or roasted. I have also made this recipe using whole cumin seeds, which adds an interesting texture.

Lentils and other pulses

The 'a load of old lentils' image has hung over vegetarian cookery for years. Yet, the current interest in peasant-style cuisines has propelled the humble lentil into some of the smartest kitchens. My kitchen may not be one of the latter but we do eat lots of lentils – and many dried beans and other pulses.

LENTILS AND MUSHROOMS IN RED WINE

Time to make: about 5 minutes
Time to cook: about 25 minutes

Serves 2

1 leek

½ garlic clove

125 g (4 oz) chestnut mushrooms

1 tablespoon olive oil

75 ml (2½ fl oz) red wine

1½ tablespoons chopped fresh parsley

½ tablespoon chopped fresh thyme

½ teaspoon Dijon mustard

3 tablespoons tomato passata

½ tablespoon vegetarian Worcestershire sauce

400 g (14 oz) can green or brown lentils

salt and freshly ground black pepper

chopped fresh parsley, to garnish

Adding the red wine to the leek, garlic and mushrooms.

Chestnut mushrooms, also known as brown mushrooms, have an intensity of flavour often lacking in the common white capped variety. I always buy them for any dish that calls for unspecified mushrooms, and tend to keep a few in a paper bag in the veg drawer of the fridge, 'just in case'. I turn them into curries or stir-fries or simply sauté them in a little olive oil and butter with a clove of garlic and some chopped fresh parsley for a quick sauce for pasta. In this dish, they make a rich-tasting stew with lentils and red wine, just the thing for a cold, wintry evening if served with creamy mashed potatoes to soak up the juices.

1   To prepare the vegetables, slice the leek, then rinse it in plenty of cold water and drain well. Crush the garlic and slice the mushrooms.
2   Heat the oil in a saucepan over a medium heat. Add the leeks and garlic and cook for 3 minutes, stirring occasionally, until the leek is softened but not browned.
3   Stir in the sliced mushrooms, turn up the heat and continue cooking for a further 5 minutes, stirring occasionally, until they are lightly browned.
4   Stir in the wine, chopped parsley and thyme, mustard, tomato passata and Worcestershire sauce and season well. Bring to the boil, then simmer for 10 minutes, stirring occasionally.
5   Meanwhile, drain and rinse the lentils. Stir the lentils into the mushroom mixture and continue simmering for a further 5 minutes to heat through completely. If there is still a lot of liquid, turn up the heat and boil the mixture rapidly to reduce. The stew should be sloppy but not swimming in liquid. Check the seasoning and garnish with parsley.

Cook's Tip
Tomato passata is simply puréed tomatoes, which come in cartons or jars and can be found with the tinned tomatoes in most supermarkets or delicatessens. If you can't find it, process tinned tomatoes with their juice in a food processor, then press them through a sieve.

LENTIL AND GRILLED RED PEPPER SALAD

Time to make: 10 to 15 minutes
Time to grill: about 5 minutes

Serves 2

½ **red pepper**

½ **red onion**

1 **garlic clove**

432 g (15 oz) can green lentils

1½ tablespoons chopped fresh
flat-leaf parsley

½ **lemon**

½ **tablespoon red wine vinegar**

2 **tablespoons olive oil**

**salt and freshly ground black
pepper**

This salad is a favourite of my eldest daughter who can be persuaded to eat practically anything that contains red peppers and garlic – not at all what I was led to expect from a six-year-old. She likes this best served on toasted country-style bread which has been rubbed with garlic and drizzled with olive oil.

1 Preheat the grill to high. To prepare the vegetables, core and seed the pepper half. Finely chop the onion and crush the garlic.
2 Arrange the pepper half, cut side down, on the grill pan and grill until the skin is blackened all over, then turn it over and continue grilling until blackened on the inside. Place the pepper in a plastic bag for 2 minutes, then skin it and dice the flesh. Place the pepper in a bowl.
3 Meanwhile, drain and rinse the lentils and add them to the pepper, along with the chopped onion, garlic and parsley.
4 Finely grate the lemon rind into another small bowl, then add the vinegar, olive oil and salt and pepper and whisk together until well mixed.
5 Pour the dressing over the lentils and stir gently until well combined, then cover and chill until ready to serve.

Note
Lentils and other pulses, with their lengthy soaking and cooking times, may not seem ideal instant supper ingredients but they play such an important role in a balanced, meat-free diet, that it would be a pity to write them off. Luckily there are excellent tinned versions of most, and although I do frequently start from scratch with the dried varieties when I have time, opening a can is easiest mid-week. If you want to substitute dried lentils or pulses in these recipes, however, 155 g (5 oz) dried weight is the rough equivalent to a 400 g (14 oz) can.

SPICED RED LENTILS WITH CABBAGE

Time to make: about 5 minutes
Time to cook: 25 to 30 minutes

Serves 2

1 small onion

1 garlic clove

250 g (8 oz) white or Savoy cabbage

2 tablespoons olive oil

1 teaspoon coriander seeds

½ teaspoon caraway seeds

125 g (4 oz) red lentils

125 ml (4 fl oz) tomato passata

315 ml (10 fl oz) vegetable stock

salt and freshly ground black pepper

chopped flat-leaf parsley, to garnish

Lentils and cabbage make a hearty satisfying partnership which I utilise in all kinds of ways. This version is lightly spiced and makes a very simple supper on a cold night; add extra stock and you can turn it into a soup. To round out the meal, I usually serve this with baked potatoes or rice.

1   To prepare the vegetables, finely slice the onion, crush the garlic and shred the cabbage.
2   Heat the oil in a saucepan over a medium heat. Add the onion and garlic and cook for 3 minutes, stirring occasionally, until the onion is softened but not browned.
3   Stir in the the coriander seeds, caraway seeds and cabbage and continue cooking for a further 5 minutes until the cabbage wilts. Meanwhile, pick over the lentils, if necessary.
4   Stir in the tomato passata, lentils, stock and salt and pepper. Bring to the boil, then cover and simmer for 15 to 20 minutes, stirring occasionally, until the lentils are tender and mushy and the mixture is thick. Add more stock or water if the lentils get too dry.
5   Check the seasoning and garnish with chopped flat-leaf parsley.

Cook's Tip
Red and green lentils are the only pulses that don't need to be pre-soaked before you can use them, so are very useful for the cook in a hurry. Green lentils also work well in this dish but will take a little longer to cook.

CREAMY PUY LENTILS WITH LEMON DRESSING

Time to make: about 5 minutes
Time to cook: about 30 minutes

Serves 2

125 g (4 oz) Puy lentils
1 garlic clove
1 small tomato
4 stoned black olives
15 g (½ oz) butter
½ lemon
½ tablespoon chopped fresh tarragon
½ teaspoon grainy mustard
1½ tablespoons crème fraîche
salt and freshly ground black pepper
chopped flat-leaf parsley, tarragon sprigs and lemon wedges, to garnish

This salad can be served hot or at room temperature – either way, it has a subtle, earthy flavour that makes a change from some of the stronger Mediterranean dishes that are so popular these days. I always use Puy lentils for simple recipes like this where the lentils are not overpowered by spices, as they have a lovely distinctive flavour and keep their shape and texture even when they are cooked.

These lentils take about half an hour to cook, so when I am preparing this after work, I put the lentils on to simmer, then put the children to bed and read them stories by which time the lentils are ready for me to finish the dish. By the way, this dish is also excellent served at room temperature.

1   Put the lentils in a saucepan over a high heat, cover with cold water and bring to the boil. Boil rapidly for 10 minutes, then lower the heat and simmer gently for about 20 minutes until they are just tender. Drain well.
2   Meanwhile, prepare the vegetables and make the dressing. Chop the garlic. Seed and chop the tomato and halve the olives.
3   While the lentils are still cooking, melt the butter in a small frying pan over a medium heat. Add the garlic and fry for about 1½ minutes, stirring occasionally, until it just begins to turn brown. Grate in the lemon rind, then stir in the juice. Add the tarragon and mustard and continue cooking for 30 seconds, stirring, then stir in the crème fraîche and plenty of salt and pepper. Bring to the boil, then stir in the drained lentils.
4   Transfer the lentils to a serving dish, garnish and serve immediately, or set aside to cool to room temperature.

Cook's Tip
Brown lentils are fine if you can't find Puy lentils, but take care not to over-cook them as they will become mushy.

Creamy Puy Lentils with Lemon Dressing

GREEN LENTILS WITH GARLIC AND CORIANDER

Time to make: about 5 minutes
Time to cook: 12 to 15 minutes

Serves 2

½ small onion

1 garlic clove

2.5 cm (1 in) piece fresh root ginger

small bunch fresh coriander

½ tablespoon sunflower oil

1 teaspoon cumin seeds

½ x 400 g (14 oz) can green lentils

½ tablespoon lemon juice

pinch cayenne pepper

salt

I cook Indian food at least once a week, normally on the nights when I come home from work not knowing what's in the fridge but confident that there will be a packet of lentils, some basmati rice and a selection of spices in the storecupboard. Mahdur Jaffrey has been my guiding light since I started cooking this way – her recipes always work perfectly and she offers lots of good advice on how to put dishes together to make a meal. Her *Indian Cookery* is one of the most used books in my kitchen and it has given me the confidence to start experimenting for myself with spices and ingredients. Serve this lentil dish with boiled rice, naan bread and a fresh onion and tomato relish. For a more elaborate meal, you can also prepare the Egg and Cauliflower Curry on page 82.

1 To prepare the vegetables, chop the onion and crush the garlic. Peel and finely chop the ginger and finely chop the coriander.
2 Heat the oil in a saucepan over a medium heat. Add the onion and garlic and cook for about 5 minutes, stirring occasionally, until the onion is softened and lightly browned. Stir in the cumin seeds and chopped ginger and cook for a further 1 minute.
3 Stir in the chopped coriander and cook until it wilts, then drain and rinse the lentils. Stir them in along with the lemon juice, cayenne pepper and salt.
4 Lower the heat and simmer for 5 minutes, stirring occasionally, until the lentils are heated through.
5 Check the seasoning and serve.

Cook's Tip
If you want to use dried lentils, substitute 155 g (5 oz) and add them to the pan after the coriander. Pour in 315 ml (10 fl oz) cold water and simmer for 34 to 40 minutes until the lentils are tender, topping up with water if necessary. Add lemon juice, cayenne pepper and seasoning, then simmer for a further 5 minutes and serve.

SPICY BEAN HOTPOT

Time to make: 5 minutes
Time to cook: about 25 minutes

Serves 2

1 onion

½ garlic clove

1 tablespoon olive oil

1 teaspoon ground cumin

200 g (7 oz) canned chopped tomatoes

1 tablespoon tomato purée

few drops Tabasco sauce

½ x 432 g (15 oz) can red kidney beans, drained

½ x 432 g (15 oz) can borlotti beans, drained

½ x 432 g (15 oz) can cannellini beans, drained

salt and freshly ground black pepper

chopped fresh parsley, to garnish

My husband, who is no mean cook himself, tested this recipe for me and has cooked it several times since for sceptical, meat-eating friends. Served with garlic bread oozing with butter and a green salad, it has transformed even the most rampant carnivore, if not into an instant convert, at least into someone willing to acknowledge that vegetarian food tastes better than they expected. For the family, I serve this with baked potatoes and a salad.

1   Slice the onion and crush the garlic.
2   Heat the olive oil in a flameproof casserole. Add the onion, garlic and cumin and cook over a medium heat for 3 minutes until softened.
3   Stir in the tomatoes, tomato purée, Tabasco sauce and seasoning to taste and simmer gently for 10 minutes, stirring occasionally.
4   Add the beans to the tomato sauce, then simmer for a further 10 to 15 minutes, until the sauce has thickened and is tomato tasting. Adjust the seasoning and sprinkle with parsley. Serve immediately.

Cook's Tip
For an attractive finish, brush thin slices of French bread with olive oil, arrange over the hotpot and grill quickly until golden brown.

FLAGEOLET BEAN AND SPRING VEGETABLE STEW

Time to make: about 5 minutes
Time to cook: about 25 minutes

Serves 2

1 small leek

½ garlic clove

60 g (2 oz) baby carrots

60 g (2 oz) baby turnips

½ small cauliflower

60 g (2 oz) green beans

1 tablespoon olive oil

220 g (7 oz) canned chopped tomatoes

60 ml (2 fl oz) dry white wine

½ tablespoon chopped fresh rosemary

155 g (5 oz) canned flageolet beans

salt and freshly ground black pepper

fresh rosemary sprigs, to garnish

This stew would once have been served only in the spring as the new vegetables came in but now baby vegetables can be found just about all year round. Yet, I still enjoy the joys of seasonal British produce, and really look forward to the visits to the local pick-your-own farm to get baby vegetables at their best. That's when I cook this to get the very best flavour.

1   To prepare the vegetables, slice the leek, then rinse it in plenty of cold water and drain well. Chop the garlic. Trim the carrots and turnips and lightly scrape the skins if they need it. Break the cauliflower in florets and halve the green beans.
2   Heat the oil in a large saucepan over a medium heat. Add the leek and garlic and cook for 3 minutes, stirring occasionally, until the leek is softened but not browned.
3   Add the carrots, turnips, tomatoes with their juices, wine, rosemary and salt and pepper. Bring to the boil, then lower the heat and simmer for 10 minutes.
4   Add the drained and rinsed flageolet beans, cauliflower florets and green beans, cover and simmer for a further 10 minutes until all the vegetables are just tender. Check the seasoning and serve immediately, garnished with rosemary.

Flageolet Bean and Spring Vegetable Stew (front) served with Spiced Chick-Peas with Spinach, see page 32.

SPICED CHICK-PEAS WITH SPINACH

Time to make: about 5 minutes
Time to cook: 25 minutes

Serves 2

185 g (6 oz) fresh leaf spinach, or 125 g (4 oz) frozen leaf spinach, thawed

½ small onion

½ garlic clove

1½ tablespoons sunflower oil

½ teaspoon grated fresh root ginger

1 teaspoon ground coriander

½ teaspoon ground cumin

pinch ground turmeric

½ dried chilli, chopped

100 g (3½ oz) canned chopped tomatoes

½ x 432 g (15 oz) can chick-peas

½ teaspoon salt

½ teaspoon garam masala

Photographed on page 31

Canned chick-peas are an essential stand-by in my kitchen and often make the basis of a quick supper dish. Here they are paired up with spinach, not only a wonderful combination of textures and tastes but also nutritionally sound. I serve this with basmati rice cooked with a little turmeric in the water, which gives it a rich yellow colour.

1   To prepare the vegetables, if you are using fresh spinach, remove the thick central veins, then finely shred the leaves. Rinse well in several changes of cold water, then shake dry. Chop the onion and crush the garlic.
2   Heat the oil in a large saucepan over a medium heat. Add the onion, garlic and ginger and cook for 5 minutes, stirring occasionally, until the onions are softened and golden.
3   Stir in the coriander, cumin, turmeric and chilli and continue cooking for 1 minute, then stir in the tomatoes and their juices and cook for 5 minutes, stirring occasionally, to give a thick sauce.
4   Add the chick-peas with their liquid, salt and garam masala, then lower the heat, cover and simmer for 10 minutes.
5   Stir in the spinach, then turn up the heat and bring the mixture to the boil and cook for a further 5 minutes until the spinach is tender and the liquid almost evaporated. Check the seasoning and serve with rice or naan bread.

Cook's Tip
If you have time or plan ahead, use 75 g (2½ oz) dried chick-peas for this dish. Soak overnight, then drain well and cook in plenty of fresh water for 1½ to 2 hours until tender. Add to the sauce with 75 ml (2½ fl oz) of the cooking liquid.

PASTA WITH CHICK-PEAS AND SAGE

Time to make: about 5 minutes
Time to cook: 25 minutes

Serves 2

½ **onion**

1 **garlic clove**

1 **celery stick**

1 **tablespoon olive oil**

220 g (7 oz) **canned chopped tomatoes**

½ **tablespoon chopped fresh sage**

220 g (7 oz) **canned chick-peas**

185 g (6 oz) **dried pasta swirls or shells**

salt and freshly ground black pepper

extra virgin olive oil and grated Parmesan cheese, to serve

This is another variation on a classic tomato sauce for pasta. The addition of chick-peas and sage turn this into a hearty, filling dish that will satisfy even the hungriest meat-eater. Get out your best extra virgin olive oil – a nice green appley one is ideal – to add a final touch of flavour.

1   To prepare the vegetables, finely chop the onion, garlic and celery.
2   Heat the oil in a medium saucepan over a low heat. Add the onion, garlic and celery and cook for 3 minutes, stirring occasionally, until softened but not browned.
3   Add the tomatoes with their juices, sage and salt and pepper and turn up the heat. Bring to the boil, then lower the heat and simmer for 15 minutes until you have a thick sauce. Drain and rinse the chick-peas, then stir them in and simmer for a further 5 minutes.
4   Meanwhile, bring a large saucepan of water to the boil over a high heat. Add the pasta and cook for 10 to 12 minutes until it is just tender. Drain well.
5   Transfer the hot pasta to a serving bowl and immediately stir in the hot sauce. Serve immediately, drizzled with extra virgin olive oil and sprinkled with Parmesan cheese.

Cook's Tip
If you can't get hold of fresh sage, I recommend you substitute fresh rosemary rather than use dried sage, as it can be rather musty and over-powering.

Pasta dishes

There can be no cooking process in the world much simpler than cooking pasta, so much so that it now appears regularly in some form or other at mealtimes in every household. Not surprisingly, this is the chapter I cook the most from. This collection of recipes shows the infinite variety of ways saucing, stir-frying and baking can transform a basic starch into so many satisfying dishes.

SPAGHETTI WITH COURGETTES, GARLIC AND CHILLI

Time to make: about 5 minutes
Time to cook: 10 to 12 minutes

Serves 2

185 g (6 oz) dried spaghetti

3 small courgettes

2 garlic cloves

1 or 2 dried red chillies

3 tablespoons olive oil

salt and freshly ground black pepper

freshly grated Parmesan cheese, to serve

This dish is the creation of my sister-in-law, Debbie, who cooks it using courgettes picked fresh from her vegetable garden. If you are not so lucky as to have such a supply, choose small courgettes with no blemishes and use them as soon as possible after buying.

1 Bring a large saucepan of water to the boil over a high heat. Add the spaghetti and cook for 10 to 12 minutes until it is just tender. Drain well.
2 Meanwhile, cut the courgettes into quarters lengthways, then slice thinly. Slice the garlic and chop the chillies.
3 Heat the oil in a frying pan over a medium heat. Add the garlic and fry briskly for 1 minute, stirring occasionally, until it is lightly browned. Remove from the pan with a slotted spoon and set aside.
4 Add the courgettes and the chillies to the pan and fry for 3 to 5 minutes, stirring occasionally, until lightly browned but still crisp. Add salt and pepper and return the garlic to the pan.
5 Transfer the drained spaghetti to a serving dish. Pour the courgettes over and toss together well. Serve immediately with grated Parmesan cheese.

Cooking Pasta
A half-Sicilian friend once gave me some basic tips for cooking pasta which I now follow with consistently excellent results. Always use a very large pan of water so that the pasta can move around as the water boils; only stir once when you add the pasta to the pan, then keep the water at a steady simmer so the pasta does not stick together, and finally, when the pasta is just al dente – still with a little bite – remove the pan from the heat and run a splash of cold water directly into the pan before draining. This stops the pasta cooking any further and sticking together, and I think is much more effective than adding a little oil to the cooking water as many books suggest.

Adding the courgettes, garlic and chillies to the freshly cooked spaghetti.

TAGLIATELLE WITH GRILLED PEPPER AND AUBERGINE

Time to make: about 5 minutes
Time to cook: 15 minutes

Serves 2

1 red pepper

1 small aubergine

1 onion

1 garlic clove

2 tablespoons extra virgin olive oil

155 g (5 oz) dried tagliatelle

½ tablespoon balsamic vinegar

90 g (3 oz) mozzarella cheese

4 fresh basil leaves

salt and freshly ground black pepper

freshly grated Parmesan, to serve

Grilling aubergines brings out their intense smoky flavour without adding too much fat, and it's a technique I use a lot as I'm a devoted aubergine fan. Properly treated, the flesh has a rich, distinctive quality that turns most people into instant fanatics. This dish is also excellent served at room temperature as a salad.

1   Preheat the grill to medium. To prepare the vegetables, halve, core and seed the pepper. Cut the aubergine in half lengthways and quarter the onion. Crush the garlic.
2   Arrange the pepper, aubergine halves and onion quarters on the grill pan, brush with 1 tablespoon of the olive oil and grill for 15 minutes, turning them over occasionally, until they are browned all over and tender.
3   Meanwhile, bring a large pan of water to the boil over a high heat. Add the pasta and cook for about 10 minutes until it is just tender.
4   Slice the grilled pepper, aubergine and onion, then put them in a bowl with the remaining 1 tablespoon olive oil. Add the vinegar and garlic and salt and pepper and toss well together.
5   Drain and cube the mozzarella and shred the basil leaves.
6   Drain the pasta and immediately put it in a large serving dish. Add the dressed vegetables, mozzarella cheese and basil and toss well together. Serve immediately with Parmesan cheese.

PASTA SHELLS WITH SPROUTING SEEDS

Time to make: about 2 minutes
Time to cook: 10 to 12 minutes

Serves 2

185 g (6 oz) dried pasta shells

1 garlic clove

60 g (2 oz) goats' cheese

2 tablespoons olive oil

2 tablespoons black olive paste

60 g (2 oz) mixed sprouting seeds and beans

salt and freshly ground black pepper

Sprouted seeds and beans make a valuable addition to a vegetarian diet, as they are rich sources of protein, fibre, vitamins and minerals. I add them to salads and sandwiches but have to admit that I buy mine in bags from supermarkets, despite repeated assurances from my colleagues that these foods are simple to grow at home!

1   Bring a large saucepan of water to the boil over a high heat. Add the pasta and cook for 10 to 12 minutes until it is just tender. Drain well and transfer to a serving bowl.
2   Meanwhile, crush the garlic and dice the goats' cheese.
3   While the pasta is still cooking, heat the oil in a small frying pan over a medium heat. Add the garlic and cook for 1 minute until lightly browned.
4   Add the cooked garlic and oil to the hot pasta with the olive paste, goats' cheese and sprouting seeds. Season well and toss gently together until well mixed. Serve immediately.

Cook's Tip
Look for jars of olive paste in larger supermarkets and specialist food shops. Different varieties are available and they are wonderful for adding to pasta as in this recipe, spread on good bread for quick snacks or pre-dinner nibbles or stirred into rice or vegetable stews.

CREAMY PASTA WITH GRILLED RED PEPPERS AND PEAS

Time to make: about 15 minutes
Time to cook: 10 to 12 minutes

Serves 2

1 large red pepper

60 g (2 oz) frozen peas

185 g (6 oz) dried casarecce

1 tablespoon olive oil

60 g (2 oz) soft cheese with herbs and garlic

2 tablespoons crème fraîche

2 tablespoons shredded fresh basil

salt and freshly ground black pepper

freshly grated Parmesan cheese, to serve

Sweet grilled peppers and peas complement each other so well in this dish – here I've suggested the pasta shape casarecce, small twisted pasta which has the grooves necessary to hold the creamy sauce, but you could also use macaroni or fusilli. Pick a soft cheese such as Boursin, which is made without rennet, and serve with a mixed leaf salad.

1   Preheat the grill to high. Place the whole pepper on the grill pan and grill for about 5 minutes, turning occasionally, until the skin is blackened on all sides. Place the pepper in a plastic bag for 2 minutes for the skin to loosen.
2   Meanwhile, cook the peas in a saucepan of boiling water for 2 minutes until just tender. Drain well, refresh under cold water and drain again.
3   Halve, core and seed the pepper, then peel off the skin. Cut the flesh into 2.5 cm (1 in) strips.
4   Bring a large saucepan of water to the boil over a high heat. Add the pasta and cook for 10 to 12 minutes until it is just tender. Drain well.
5   While the pasta is cooking, heat the olive oil in a large frying pan over a medium heat. Add the pepper strips and cook for 1 minute, stirring occasionally, then stir in the soft cheese and crème fraîche and continue stirring to give a smooth, creamy sauce. Add the peas and salt and pepper, then turn up the heat and bring to the boil.
6   Add the pasta and the shredded basil and toss together well to coat the pasta in the sauce. Transfer to warmed dishes and serve with grated Parmesan cheese.

Creamy Pasta with Grilled Red Peppers and Peas

FUSILLI WITH ROQUEFORT AND WALNUTS

Time to make: about 5 minutes
Time to cook: 10 to 12 minutes

Serves 2

---

185 g (6 oz) dried fusilli

90 g (3 oz) Roquefort cheese

30 g (1 oz) walnut pieces

2 tablespoons sweet white wine or white port

2 tablespoons crème fraîche

salt and freshly ground black pepper

chopped fresh flat-leaf parsley, to garnish

You can use any creamy blue cheese for this richly flavoured pasta dish but I confess to a passion for the most expensive, Roquefort. Still, a little of it goes a long way and its distinctive salty tang makes all the difference in this recipe.

As I always have to have some form of vegetable with my food (fruit will do at breakfast!), I serve this with steamed broccoli or a spinach salad.

1   Bring a large saucepan of water to the boil over a high heat. Add the pasta and cook for 10 to 12 minutes until it is just tender. Drain well and transfer to a serving bowl.
2   Meanwhile, dice the Roquefort cheese and finely chop the walnut pieces.
3   While the pasta is still cooking, put the wine and cream in a small pan and heat until it is just boiling. Lower the heat, stir in the Roquefort cheese and continue stirring until the cheese melts and the sauce is the consistency of single cream. Season to taste with salt and pepper.
4   Stir the walnuts into the sauce, then pour it over the hot pasta and toss together gently until all the pasta is well coated. Sprinkle the parsley over the top and serve immediately.

Cook's Tip
I nearly always use dried pasta and keep a selection of shapes to hand. To get the best shape for the sauce, use the following guide – the thinner and runnier the sauce the longer the pasta, so use short, stubby shapes for thicker, chunkier sauces.

WARM PASTA AND PESTO SALAD

Time to make: about 10 minutes,
 plus cooling
Time to cook: 10 to 12 minutes

Serves 2

185 g (6 oz) dried pasta shells

**1½ tablespoons ready-made
pesto sauce**

1 tablespoon olive oil

2 plum tomatoes

2 spring onions

60 g (2 oz) feta cheese

**1 tablespoon pine nuts,
optional**

8 stoned black olives

**salt and freshly ground black
pepper**

I keep a tub of ready-made pesto permanently in the fridge and add it to all kinds of dishes. To pass it off as the real thing, I add extra fresh basil and really good olive oil just before serving, and feel just like the lady in the television advertisement who doesn't admit that she's serving a shop-bought pie!

1 Bring a large saucepan of water to the boil over a high heat. Add the pasta and cook for 10 to 12 minutes until it is just tender. Drain well and place in a large bowl.
2 Add the pesto and olive oil to the pasta and mix together well. Set aside for 15 minutes to cool to room temperature.
3 Meanwhile, prepare the vegetables and cheese. Seed and chop the tomatoes. Chop the spring onions. Cube the feta cheese.
4 If you are using the pine nuts, heat a small frying pan over a high heat. Add the pine nuts and dry fry until they are golden, then immediately turn them out of the pan to stop the cooking.
5 Add the tomatoes, cheese, spring onions and olives to the pasta and mix together well. Season with salt and pepper and sprinkle with the pine nuts if you are using. Serve with ciabatta bread to mop up any extra dressing.

Cook's Tip
Ready-made pesto is now widely available, and the fresh versions from chill cabinets are far superior to most of the pesto sold in jars. If you cannot find a brand you like, however, make a large batch yourself and freeze it in ice-cube trays. Then you can use a cube at a time as you need it.

CHINESE-STYLE NOODLES WITH BROCCOLI AND SESAME

Time to make: about 5 minutes
Time to cook: about 15 minutes

Serves 2

250 g (8 oz) broccoli

1 garlic clove

2.5 cm (1 in) piece fresh root ginger

1 dried red chilli

125 g (4 oz) baby corn

185 g (6 oz) Chinese noodles

2 tablespoons tahini paste

1 tablespoon dark soy sauce

1 tablespoon red wine vinegar

1 tablespoon dark muscovado sugar

1 tablespoon sunflower oil

1 tablespoon sesame seeds

I use Chinese rice noodles in this recipe but tagliatelle works just as well, and I have also made it with egg noodles. This sesame sauce works well with any combination of vegetables but I particularly like the colour and texture combination of broccoli and baby corn.

1 To prepare the vegetables, cut the broccoli into florets. Chop the garlic, peel and chop the ginger and chop the chilli.
2 Bring a large saucepan of water to the boil over a high heat. Add the broccoli and corn and return the water to the boil, then remove the vegetables from the pan with a slotted spoon and plunge into cold water. Drain and pat dry with kitchen paper.
3 Add the noodles to the pan and cook for 5 minutes until tender. Drain and run under cold water to cool, then drain again.
4 Meanwhile, put the tahini paste, soy sauce, vinegar and sugar in a bowl and mix together, then set aside.
5 Heat the oil in a wok or large frying pan over a high heat until almost smoking. Add the garlic, ginger and chilli and stir-fry for 30 seconds, then add the broccoli and corn and continue stir-frying for 3 minutes.
6 Add the noodles to the pan along with the tahini mixture and stir together for 2 minutes until completely heated through. Sprinkle with sesame seeds and serve immediately.

Cook's Tip
Tahini paste is made from sesame seeds and comes in two versions, dark and light. The only difference is that, in the dark variety, the seeds have been toasted which intensifies the nutty flavour. If your tahini has oil floating on top stir it through the paste before using as the excess oil will affect the texture of the final sauce.

Chinese-style Noodles with Broccoli and Sesame

GNOCCHI WITH CREAMED TOMATO AND BASIL SAUCE

Time to make: about 10 minutes
Time to cook: about 20 minutes

Serves 2

200 g (6½ oz) packet potato gnocchi

Sauce

1 shallot

1 small carrot

1 stick celery

2 tablespoons sunflower or vegetable oil

200 g (6½ oz) can chopped tomatoes

2 tablespoons chopped fresh basil

3 tablespoons double cream

salt and freshly ground black pepper

fresh basil leaves, to garnish

freshly grated Parmesan cheese, to serve

This is an immensely useful sauce that I make up in batches minus the cream and freeze for use in all kinds of dishes. I serve it on pasta, add vegetables for a stew, or simmer it until it is really thick to use as a topping for pizzas. Whilst I was writing this book, commercially prepared potato gnocchi became available and have since occupied a permanent place in my fridge, as I love gnocchi but never have time to make them by hand. The shop-bought versions can be a little heavy but very acceptable as a quick supper dish when served with a sauce such as this.

1   To prepare the vegetables for the sauce, chop the shallot and finely chop the carrot and celery.
2   Heat the oil in a small saucepan over a low heat. Add the shallot, carrot and celery and cook for 5 minutes until softened.
3   Stir in the tomatoes with their juices, basil and salt and pepper. Bring to the boil, then lower the heat and simmer for 15 minutes, stirring occasionally, until the liquid has reduced to form a thick sauce.
4   Place the sauce in a blender or processor and whiz for 2 minutes until smooth, then return to the cleaned pan. Stir in the cream and re-heat gently but do not allow to boil. Check the seasoning.
5   Meanwhile, to cook the gnocchi, bring a large pan of salted water to the boil and cook over high heat. Add the gnocchi and cook until the gnocchi rise to the surface of the water.
6   Drain thoroughly, then place the gnocchi in a serving dish and pour over the sauce. Garnish with fresh basil and serve.

Cook's Tip
To freeze the sauce, omit the cream and leave to cool completely. Transfer to a rigid container, cover and freeze for up to 1 month. To use, re-heat slowly from frozen, then stir in the cream.

PASTA SHELLS
WITH BLACK OLIVE PASTE

Time to make: 5 minutes
Time to cook: 10 to 12 minutes

Serves 2

185 g (6 oz) pasta shells

30 g (1 oz) pine nuts

1 tablespoon black olive paste

3 tablespoon shredded fresh basil

2 tablespoons olive oil

3 tablespoons grated pecorino cheese

salt and freshly ground black pepper

Ready-made olive pastes now appear on many supermarket and delicatessen shelves, but take care when buying as they can vary greatly in quality. Look for ones made from only olives, good-quality olive oil and just a few added herbs; some brands use sunflower oil and all kinds of flavourings and lose intensity as a result.

This recipe fits this book perfectly as it's entirely made from storecupboard ingredients, having been created on one of those nights when the (fresh veg) cupboard really was bare.

1 Bring a large saucepan of water to the boil over a high heat. Add the pasta and cook for 10 to 12 minutes until tender.
2 Meanwhile, place the pine nuts in a small frying pan over a medium heat and dry-fry for 1 to 2 minutes until golden.
3 Drain the pasta well and transfer it to a large serving bowl. Add the toasted pine nuts, black olive paste, basil, olive oil and pecorino cheese and toss together gently. Season to taste and serve immediately.

Cook's Tip
To prevent an opened container of olive paste from going off, always cover the surface with extra olive oil, then cover and store in a cool, dark place.

STIR-FRIED GREENS WITH TOFU AND NOODLES

Time to make: 5 minutes
Time to cook: 20 to 25 minutes

Serves 2

125 g (4 oz) Chinese egg noodles

125 g (4 oz) marinated or smoked tofu

1 garlic clove

2.5 cm (1 in) piece fresh root ginger

4 spring onions

250 g (8 oz) spring greens

1 carrot

vegetable oil for deep-frying

2 tablespoons sunflower oil

3 tablespoons dark soy sauce

1 tablespoon dark muscovado sugar

1 tablespoon red wine vinegar

1 tablespoon sesame oil

Tofu can be delicious when treated properly but many people are put off at the first attempt by the bland taste and somewhat flabby texture. I find marinating it and then roasting or deep-frying it makes it far more palatable, or you could try the smoked variety. Be careful with seasoning, though, as smoked tofu can be very salty.

1 Bring a large saucepan of water to the boil over a high heat. Add the noodles and cook according to packet instructions. Drain, run under cold water and drain again, then set aside.
2 Meanwhile, cut the tofu into 5 cm (2 in) cubes. To prepare the vegetables, crush the garlic. Peel and chop the ginger. Slice the spring onions. Shred the spring greens and halve the carrot lengthways and then slice it.
3 Heat about 5 cm (2 in) vegetable oil in a wok or small deep frying pan over a high heat. Add the tofu cubes in batches and deep-fry for 2 to 3 minutes until golden.
4 Remove the cubes from the wok or pan with a slotted spoon and drain well on kitchen paper.
5 Heat the sunflower oil in the cleaned wok or in a large frying pan over a high heat. Add the garlic and ginger and stir-fry for 1 minute. Add the spring onions, greens and carrot and continue stir-frying for a further 5 minutes until the vegetables are wilted.
6 Put the soy sauce in a bowl and stir in the sugar and vinegar along with 4 tablespoons water.
7 Add the noodles to the wok or frying pan and stir-fry for 1 to 2 minutes, then sprinkle over the soy sauce mixture and continue stir-frying for a further 2 minutes. Add the sesame oil, stir well to mix and serve immediately.

Stir-fried Greens with Tofu and Noodles

RICE NOODLES WITH COCONUT AND THAI SPICES

Time to make: about 5 minutes
Time to cook: 20 to 25 minutes

Serves 2

185 g (6 oz) medium rice noodles

1 small onion

1 garlic clove

125 g (4 oz) marinated or smoked tofu

60 g (2 oz) shiitake or chestnut mushrooms

1 stick celery

1 tablespoon sunflower oil

1 tablespoon Thai green curry paste

155 ml (5 fl oz) vegetable stock

220 ml (7 fl oz) coconut milk

chopped fresh coriander, to garnish

Rice noodles are the slightly transparent looking ones you find in oriental supermarkets. They take very little time to cook and are lighter in texture and less filling than Italian wheat noodles, which makes them so suited to the clean flavours of Thai cooking. My husband enjoys cooking this dish and he starts from scratch with fresh lemon grass, chillies and ginger, but mid-week I just use a tablespoon of a ready-made Thai curry paste from the supermarket. If you enjoy cooking Thai food, there are specialist shops setting up in larger towns all over the country where you can find most, if not all, of the ingredients you need. They are also available by mail order, so check the list at the end of the book, see page 95.

1   Bring a large saucepan of water to the boil over a high heat. Add the noodles and cook for 6 to 10 minutes until tender. Drain and transfer to a bowl of cold water while preparing the rest of the dish – this will stop the noodles from becoming sticky.
2   Meanwhile, slice the onion and chop the garlic. Cube the tofu and slice the mushrooms and celery.
3   Heat the oil in a saucepan over a medium heat. Add the onion and garlic and cook for 5 minutes, stirring occasionally, until the onion slices are golden. Stir in the curry paste and cook for a further 3 minutes, stirring constantly. Stir in the stock, lower the heat and simmer for 5 minutes.
4   Stir in the coconut milk, turn up the heat and bring to the boil, then stir in the tofu and mushrooms with the drained noodles. Allow to heat through completely, scatter with the sliced celery and chopped coriander and serve.

TAGLIATELLE WITH ASPARAGUS AND SUN-DRIED TOMATO

Time to make: 5 minutes
Time to cook: 10 minutes

Serves 2

175 g (6 oz) fresh tagliatelle

125 g (4 oz) asparagus tips

2 sun-dried tomatoes in oil, drained

1 tablespoon walnut oil

4 tablespoons dry white wine

2 egg yolks

4 tablespoons double cream or crème fraîche

30 g (1 oz) freshly grated Parmesan cheese

salt and freshly ground black pepper

This recipe sounds incredibly smart and expensive, but is actually nothing of the kind. Asparagus tips are available just about all year round now, though I prefer to wait for the short English season in May to really enjoy asparagus at its best. Sun-dried tomatoes, despite being saddled with a very trendy reputation, are actually tasty and a welcome addition to any storecupboard. Use the ones preserved in oil for this dish as they are ready to use and don't need lengthy pre-soaking.

1   Bring a large saucepan of water to the boil over a high heat. Add the pasta and cook for 5 minutes until just tender.
2   While the pasta is cooking, bring another pan of water to the boil. Add the asparagus tips and blanch for 1 minute. Immediately drain and refresh the tips under cold water, then drain again. Pat dry with kitchen paper.
3   Meanwhile, finely chop the sun-dried tomatoes. Heat the walnut oil in a large saucepan over a medium heat. Add the asparagus tips and sun-dried tomatoes and fry for 2 minutes, stirring occasionally. Stir in the wine and salt and pepper, lower the heat and simmer until the wine reduces by half.
4   Put the egg yolks in a bowl and beat in the cream or crème fraîche and the Parmesan cheese.
5   Add the drained pasta to the asparagus tips and mix together well. Stir in the cream and egg mixture, then continue stirring over a low heat until the sauce just thickens. Check the seasoning and serve immediately.

Cook's Tip
Walnut oil adds a distinctive flavour to this dish – I keep a bottle for adding to dressings and for use in breadmaking. It's particularly good in tea breads. Buy it at large supermarkets or delicatessens and store it in a dark, cool place.

Vegetable dishes and salads

During the last ten years there has been an enormous increase in the variety of fresh fruit and vegetables available. When cooking from this chapter, however, I hope you choose recipes that use ingredients that are in season naturally. Not only are they likely to be at their peak, they will taste better.

BAKED FLAT MUSHROOMS WITH GOATS' CHEESE

Time to make: about 5 minutes
Time to cook: 15 minutes

Serves 2

4 large flat mushrooms

2 teaspoons black olive paste

4 thin slices goats' cheese, about 125 g (4 oz)

1 tablespoon pine nuts

2 tablespoons olive oil

2 or 3 fresh basil leaves

salt and freshly ground black pepper

On the rare occasions that I have an evening alone when my husband Mark is out and the children are asleep, I tend to opt out and just have a boiled egg on a tray. Whilst writing this book, however, I've felt more inspired to cook something special just for myself but the requirements of such a dish are these – practically no preparation and ingredients that happen to be in the fridge. On one particular night some flat mushrooms and goats' cheese produced this, which was so good I promptly cooked it for friends the following night as a starter. Walnut bread and thin green beans are all you need to round out the meal.

1 Preheat the oven to 200°C, 400°F, Gas 6. To prepare the mushrooms, remove the stalks.
2 Spread the dark inside of the mushroom caps with olive paste. Place on an oiled baking sheet.
3 Arrange a slice of goats' cheese on each mushroom, scatter with pine nuts and drizzle with olive oil. Season with salt and pepper.
4 Bake the mushrooms for 15 minutes until the cheese is melted and golden. Meanwhile, shred the basil leaves.
5 Scatter over the shredded basil and serve.

Cook's Tip
Pick a rinded goats' cheese with a diameter similar to that of the mushrooms for this quick dish. It should sit neatly within each mushroom's cap.

Ready to serve Baked Flat Mushrooms with Goats' Cheese.

SUMMER VEGETABLE BAKE

Time to make: about 5 minutes
Time to cook: about 25 minutes

Serves 2

3 courgettes

8 cherry tomatoes

1 small aubergine

1 garlic clove

3 tablespoons extra virgin olive oil

45 g (1½ oz) fresh breadcrumbs

3 tablespoons chopped fresh flat-leaf parsley

salt and freshly ground black pepper

When fresh vegetables are at their peak, they need little enhancement as the wonderful flavours work together to make a satisfying dish on their own. Last summer I grew a single courgette plant in a grow bag and the results were used to great effect in this simple recipe. If you add a tumbling tomato plant to your patio display, you can have the tomatoes freshly picked as well.

1   Preheat the oven to 200°C, 400°F, Gas 6. To prepare the vegetables, cut the courgettes into 5 cm (2 in) wedges, halve the tomatoes and halve and slice the aubergine. Chop the garlic.
2   Place the courgettes, tomatoes and aubergine together in a bowl, then add the oil and salt and pepper and toss to coat the vegetables in the oil. Arrange in an oiled gratin dish large enough to take all the vegetables in a single layer.
3   Bake for about 20 minutes, basting with oil and juices, until the vegetables are golden.
4   Meanwhile, put the crumbs in a small bowl and stir in the garlic and parsley.
5   Spoon the mixture over the vegetable juices to soak up the juices, then return the dish to the oven for 5 minutes until golden. Serve with crusty bread to mop up any juices.

Cook's Tip
Add fresh basil and mozzarella slices to make this a more substantial supper dish. Simply slice 90 g (3 oz) buffalo mozzarella cheese and tuck the slices between the vegetables. Add a couple of tablespoons of chopped fresh basil to the topping and cook as above.

SPICED VEGETABLE PANCAKES

Time to make: 10 to 15 minutes
Time to cook: 10 to 15 minutes

Serves 2

125 g (4 oz) new potatoes

½ small onion

¼ fresh green chilli

1 small tomato

½ tablespoon sunflower oil

½ teaspoon grated fresh root ginger

½ teaspoon cumin seeds

½ teaspoon garam masala

½ tablespoon lemon juice

125 g (4 oz) frozen mixed vegetables, thawed

salt

Pancakes

125 g (4 oz) gram flour

¼ teaspoon cayenne pepper

¼ teaspoon salt

pinch bicarbonate of soda

1 tablespoon chopped fresh coriander

sunflower oil for frying

Gram flour is made from chick-peas, which gives it a delicious nutty flavour that makes excellent savoury pancakes. I also use it to make vegetable fritters, which go down well with the whole family. If you are not adept at making pancakes, you can use ready-made crêpes or flour tortillas which are now available in many supermarkets and delicatessens. Look for gram flour in Indian or health food shops and large supermarkets.

1   Bring a large saucepan of water to the boil over a high heat. Add the potatoes and cook for 10 minutes until tender.
2   Meanwhile, slice the onion. Seed and chop the chilli and chop the tomato.
3   When the potatoes are tender, drain them throughly, then cut them into cubes. Set aside while you prepare the filling.
4   Heat the oil in a saucepan over a medium heat. Add the onion, ginger, chilli and cumin seeds and cook for 3 minutes, stirring occasionally, until the onions are softened.
5   Stir in the garam masala, lemon juice and salt and cook for a further 30 seconds, stirring. Stir in the potatoes, vegetables and tomato and continue cooking, stirring, for 5 minutes. Keep warm while cooking the pancakes.
6   To make the pancakes, sift the gram flour with the cayenne pepper, salt and bicarbonate of soda into a bowl. Whisk in 440 ml (14 fl oz) cold water to give a smooth batter. Stir in the coriander.
7   Heat a little oil in a 20 cm (8 in) frying pan over a medium heat. Add a ladleful of batter and cook until lightly browned, then use a metal spatula to turn over and continue cooking the other side until it is lightly browned. Remove from the pan and keep warm while you repeat with the remaining batter to make 3 more pancakes.
8   Divide the vegetable mixture between the pancakes, fold over and serve.

Cook's Tip
These pancakes can be made in advance and warmed through, covered with foil, in a low oven.

BRAISED AUBERGINE WITH THAI SPICES

Time to make: about 5 minutes
Time to cook: about 25 minutes

Serves 2

250 g (8 oz) aubergine

1 small onion

1 garlic clove

1 cm (½ in) piece fresh root ginger

1½ tablespoons sunflower oil

½ tablespoon red curry paste

1½ tablespoons fresh lime juice

1 tablespoon dark muscovado sugar

½ teaspoon black bean sauce

salt

8 fresh basil leaves (use Thai basil if you can get it)

finely shredded lime rind, to garnish

As anyone who has read through this book will have realised, aubergine (along with grilled red peppers) makes a very regular appearance in the Gwynn household in one form or other. This recipe must be one of my favourites, as the sweet-and-sour Thai sauce really complements both the texture and smoky taste of the vegetable. What's more, it is incredibly simple to prepare, cooks in no time and is just as good cold – in fact, I think this is one of the best recipes in the book. I like to eat this with Thai fragrant rice.

1   To prepare the vegetables, cube the aubergines, slice the onion and chop the garlic. Chop the ginger.
2   Heat the oil in a wok or large frying pan over a medium heat. Add the onion, garlic and ginger and stir-fry for 3 minutes until just beginning to brown.
3   Stir in the curry paste and cook for 1 minute. Add the aubergine cubes and stir-fry for about 3 minutes until they are lightly browned.
4   Stir in the lime juice, sugar, black bean sauce, salt to taste and 315 ml (10 fl oz) cold water and bring to the boil, stirring. Lower the heat, cover and simmer for 15 minutes until the aubergine is tender.
5   Remove the pan lid and continue simmering the mixture until the liquid is reduced and the sauce is thick and syrupy. Stir in the basil, garnish and serve immediately.

Cook's Tips
Red curry paste is easily available in oriental supermarkets and specialist shops. It can be very hot so use sparingly if it's a brand you have not tried before.

Thai basil, also called holy basil, is particularly aromatic and stands up to the strong flavours used here. You will find it in Asian supermarkets.

Braised Aubergine with Thai Spices served with rice.

SWEET POTATO HASH

Time to make: about 5 minutes
Time to cook: about 20 minutes,
  plus grilling

Serves 2

185 g (6 oz) sweet potato

185 g (6 oz) potato

1 small leek

½ small onion

1½ tablespoons olive oil

pinch ground ginger

1½ tablespoons chopped fresh
flat-leaf parsley

30 g (1 oz) Gruyère cheese

salt and freshly ground black
pepper

I really started buying sweet potatoes on a regular basis when I discovered them as the perfect starchy vegetable for weaning my daughters, who both preferred them to ordinary potatoes. The girls still enjoy them but in dishes like this hash, as opposed to puréed! Try to get the pink-fleshed potatoes if you can – they look far more attractive than the slightly green-fleshed ones which go grey when cooked.

1   Bring 2 saucepans of water to the boil over a high heat. While they are heating, cube both kinds of potatoes. Add the potatoes to the boiling water and cook for 10 minutes until tender. Drain thoroughly, then place in a large mixing bowl and mash both together.
2   Meanwhile, thinly slice the leek, rinse in plenty of cold water and drain throughly. Thinly slice the onion.
3   Heat 1 tablespoon of the oil in a frying pan with a flameproof handle over a medium heat. Add the leek and onion and cook for 5 minutes until softened and lightly browned. Add to the potatoes, along with the ginger, parsley and plenty of salt and pepper and mix together well.
4   Heat the remaining oil in the cleaned frying pan over a medium heat until very hot. Add the potato mixture and fry for 5 minutes until heated through and beginning to brown. Flatten the potato into a cake with the back of the spoon and cook until the base is golden and crisp.
5   Meanwhile, preheat the grill and grate the cheese. Scatter the cheese over the top of the hash and grill for 3 to 4 minutes until bubbling and golden. Serve immediately, cut into wedges, with a green vegetable.

Cook's Tip
Shredded cabbage makes a good addition to this dish; however, when I do add it, I replace the ground ginger with caraway seeds.

MUSHROOM AND COCONUT CURRY

Time to make: about 3 minutes
Time to cook: about 20 minutes

Serves 2

250 g (8 oz) chestnut mushrooms

1 small onion

½ clove garlic

1 tablespoon vegetable oil

½ teaspoon chopped fresh root ginger

¼ teaspoon ground cumin

½ teaspoon ground coriander

pinch turmeric

pinch cayenne pepper

7 g (¼ oz) creamed coconut

3 tablespoons Greek-style yogurt

½ teaspoon salt

¼ teaspoon garam masala

½ tablespoon lemon juice

Apparently mushrooms aren't traditionally used in Indian cookery, so mushroom curries are relative newcomers to the scene. About five years ago I came across a particularly tasty mushroom curry subtly flavoured with coconut at the Kalpna restaurant in Edinburgh; that inspired this recipe which makes a wonderful quick supper served with basmati rice and a lentil daal.

1 To prepare the vegetables, halve the mushrooms and finely chop the onion and garlic.
2 Heat the oil in a saucepan over a low heat. Add the garlic, ginger and onion and cook for 5 minutes, stirring occasionally, until they are softened.
3 Stir in the the cumin, coriander, turmeric and cayenne pepper and continue cooking for 1 minute. Add the mushrooms, cover and cook for 10 minutes until the mushrooms are softened.
4 Meanwhile, put the creamed coconut in a small bowl and dissolve with 1 to 2 tablespoons water to form a thick paste. Stir into the mushrooms along with the yogurt, salt and garam masala, then continue simmering for 5 minutes until the sauce is the consistency of thick cream.
5 Stir in the lemon juice and serve immediately.

Cook's Tip
Creamed coconut comes in a hard block which has to be reconstituted with water to make coconut milk. Crumble the creamed coconut into small pieces and then mash with a little water to give a thick cream, then thin down as desired. Substitute canned coconut milk if you wish.

BABY SPINACH & BROAD BEAN SALAD WITH GARLIC CROÛTONS

Time to make: about 10 minutes
Time to cook: 5 to 8 minutes

Serves 2 to 3

1 kg (2 lb) fresh broad beans in their pods

6 spring onions

125 g (4 oz) feta cheese

200 g (6½ oz) fresh baby spinach

1 tablespoon chopped fresh mint

1 tablespoon white wine vinegar

3 tablespoons extra virgin olive oil

salt and freshly ground pepper

Croûtons

1 large slice white country bread

1 garlic clove

2 tablespoons olive oil

Broad beans are one of those vegetables which really bring home the pleasures of eating with the seasons. As far as I am concerned they are only really worth eating fresh, preferably just picked, as the greyish skin which coats each bean becomes tough when the beans get too large or are frozen. Broad beans (along with fresh raspberries) are one of the main reasons I patronise the local pick-your-own farm; freshly picked, blanched in boiling water and tossed in a salad, they are a true taste of summer for me.

1   To prepare the vegetables, shell the broad beans; you should end up with about 250 g (8 oz) shelled weight. Chop the spring onions. Cube the feta cheese.
2   To prepare the croûtons, cut the bread into large cubes and crush the garlic.
3   Bring a saucepan of water to the boil over a high heat. Add the beans and cook for 2 minutes until just tender. Drain, refresh under cold water and drain again. Pat dry with kitchen paper.
4   Place the beans in a salad bowl with the spinach, spring onions and feta cheese.
5   To make a dressing, put the mint, vinegar, oil and salt and pepper in a small bowl and whisk until well combined.
6   To make the croûtons, heat the oil in a small frying pan over a medium heat. Add the bread cubes and garlic and stir-fry until they are golden. Remove the croûtons from the pan with a slotted spoon and drain well on kitchen paper. Sprinkle with salt.
7   Add the croûtons to the salad with the dressing, toss gently to coat the salad leaves in oil and serve immediately with pieces of crusty bread.

Cook's Tip
If using frozen beans, blanch them, then slip off the grey skins before adding to the salad.

Baby Spinach & Broad Bean Salad with Garlic Croûtons

GADO-GADO

Time to make: about 10 minutes
Time to cook: about 15 minute

Serves 2 to 3

185 g (6 oz) small new
potatoes

1 carrot, about 125 g (4 oz)

185 g (6 oz) fine green beans

185 g (6 oz) white cabbage

¼ cucumber

125 g (4 oz) fresh bean sprouts

Peanut Sauce

1 garlic clove

1 teaspoon sunflower oil

4 tablespoons crunchy peanut
butter

1 tablespoon dark soy sauce

1 teaspoon dark muscovado
sugar

1 tablespoon lemon juice

½ teaspoon chilli paste

4 tablespoons coconut milk

This is my version of the increasingly popular Indonesian vegetable salad. It's the only way I can get my husband Mark to eat peanut butter, which he normally considers a complete abomination. The sauce also goes well with vegetable kebabs, served satay style.

1   Bring 2 saucepans of water to the boil over high heat. Add the potatoes to one and cook for 10 minutes until tender. Drain, refresh under cool water and drain again. Pat dry with kitchen paper.
2   Meanwhile, peel and cut the carrots into matchsticks, halve the green beans, shred the cabbage and cut the cucumber into matchsticks.
3   Add the carrot and green beans to the other pan, return to the boil and cook for 3 minutes, adding the cabbage for the last minute – the vegetables should still be crisp. Drain, refresh in a bowl of cold water and drain again. Pat dry with kitchen paper.
4   Place the cooked vegetables in a large salad bowl, add the bean sprouts and cucumber and gently toss together.
5   To prepare the sauce, crush the garlic. Heat the oil in a small pan over a medium heat. Add the garlic and cook for 1 minute until golden. Stir in the peanut butter and 4 tablespoons cold water until well blended.
6   Off the heat, stir in the soy sauce, sugar, lemon juice and chilli paste, then return the pan to the heat and simmer, stirring, to give a smooth sauce.
7   Stir in the coconut milk, heat through and pour over the salad. Toss gently and serve.

CELERIAC AND CARROT REMOULADE

Time to make: 10 to 15 minutes

Serves 2

185 g (6 oz) celeriac

185 g (6 oz) carrot

½ tablespoon capers

1 tablespoon lemon juice

chopped flat-leaf parsley, to garnish

Mustard Mayonnaise

1 egg yolk, size 6

1 teaspoon Dijon mustard

90 ml (3 fl oz) olive oil

1 tablespoon lemon juice

a little milk, optional

salt and freshly ground black pepper

My parents-in-law live in the north of France and, when we visit them, my husband's mother stocks up on celeriac remoulade from her local delicatessen or supermarket. This simple combination of root vegetables with a mustard-flavoured mayonnaise is great as a starter on picnics, and is a family favourite. Because it is not widely available in this country and I have to make it, I add carrot for sweetness and a few capers for extra bite.

1 To prepare the vegetables, peel and coarsely grate the celeriac and carrot or cut them into very thin matchsticks.
2 Place the celeriac and carrot in a bowl with the capers and lemon juice and mix well to combine.
3 To make the mustard mayonnaise, place the egg yolk in a small bowl with the mustard and salt and pepper and mix together well. Gradually dribble in the olive oil, whisking contantly, until the mixture becomes thick and creamy. Stir in the lemon juice and, if the mayonnaise is too thick, add a little milk to give a coating consistency. Check the seasoning.
4 Pour the mayonnaise over the vegetables and toss gently to coat in the dressing. Transfer to a serving dish, sprinkle with parsley and serve.

Rice and grain dishes

Go into any food shop these days, head for the rice section and marvel at the selection of rices available in even the smallest shop. One of the joys of cooking with these rice varieties is discovering their different properties and using them in dishes that make the most of these differences.

POLENTA WITH MUSHROOM SAUCE

Time to make: 10 minutes
Time to cook: about 20 minutes

Serves 2

185 g (6 oz) instant polenta

15 g (½ oz) butter

30 g (1 oz) freshly grated Parmesan cheese

salt and freshly ground black pepper

Sauce

15 g (½ oz) dried porcini mushrooms

1 shallot

125 g (4 oz) chestnut mushrooms

2 tablespoons olive oil

155 ml (5 fl oz) tomato passata

2 tablespoons chopped fresh flat-leaf parsley

2 tablespoons dry white wine

Butter and cheese being added to the polenta mixture.

Polenta is one of those dishes that has become very trendy with the new wave of Mediterranean peasant-style cookery. It can be disappointingly bland but, with plenty of cheese and butter to give the maize flavour, it makes an excellent supper dish. I like to leave the cooked polenta to harden and then cut it into slices, and fry or grill the slices to give them a little texture. Served with a richly flavoured sauce such as this one, polenta makes a colourful meal at any time of the year.

1 First prepare the sauce. Place the dried mushrooms in a small bowl, pour over enough hot water to cover and leave to soak for 10 minutes.
2 Meanwhile, chop the shallot and slice the mushrooms. Heat the oil in a saucepan over a high heat. Add the shallot and chestnut mushrooms and cook for 5 minutes, stirring occasionally, until they are softened.
3 Drain the porcini, reserving the soaking liquid, then chop the mushrooms. Add them to the pan along with the tomato passata, parsley, white wine and reserved soaking liquid. Season with salt and pepper, turn down the heat to medium and simmer for 10 minutes until you have a thick sauce.
4 For the polenta, place 750 ml (24 fl oz) cold water in a large pan over a high heat and bring to the boil. Add ½ teaspoon salt and pour in the polenta, stirring constantly. Lower the heat and simmer for 5 to 8 minutes, stirring constantly until the polenta is thick and coming away from the sides of the pan. Stir in the butter and cheese.
5 Divide the polenta between individual dishes and top with the mushroom sauce. Serve immediately.

Cook's Tip
To grill or fry polenta, tip cooked polenta into an oiled shallow tin and spread out to a thickness of about 1 cm (½ in). Leave to cool, then cut into squares or triangles. Brush with olive oil and grill or fry until golden and crisp on each side. Serve with extra cheese or as a wonderful topping for a vegetable casserole.

SPICY RICE

Time to make: about 5 minutes
Time to cook: about 25 minutes

Serves 2

½ small onion

½ garlic clove

1 small courgette

60 g (2 oz) green beans

½ medium aubergine

1 canned pimiento, drained

1 small tomato

2 tablespoons olive oil

2 teaspoons paprika

125 g (4 oz) risotto rice

315 ml (10 fl oz) vegetable
stock, boiling

salt and freshly ground black
pepper

chopped fresh parsley, to garnish

This recipe is a family favourite; in fact, it was christened 'spicy' by my eldest daughter, although we can't work out why as it isn't really very spicy at all. Anyway the name has stuck and I find it a great way to get my children to eat vegetables, such as courgette, that would be turned down if presented in more recognisable form. It is, however, a recipe that comes close to overstepping the thirty-minute mark but the preparation involved is so simple it fits in spirit if not minutes!

1   To prepare the vegetables, chop the onion, garlic and courgette. Cut the green beans into short lengths and cube the aubergine. Chop the pimiento and tomato.
2   Heat the oil in a large saucepan over a medium heat. Add the onion and garlic and cook for 3 minutes, stirring occasionally, until softened but not browned.
3   Stir in the courgette, beans, aubergine and pimiento, turn up the heat and continue cooking for a further 5 minutes, stirring occasionally, until the vegetables are lightly browned.
4   Stir in the paprika, tomato and rice, turn down the heat and continue cooking for 1 minute. Add the stock and seasoning, turn up the heat and bring to the boil, stirring occasionally.
5   Lower the heat, cover and simmer for 15 to 20 minutes until the rice is just tender. Leave the covered pan to stand for about 5 minutes, then fork up the rice and garnish with chopped parsley.

About Rices
The Italians and Spanish, with their distinctive risottos and paellas, both use very similar short-grained rices that produces the creamy texture so prized in these dishes; Valencia rice from Spain is not so readily available in this country so I use risotto rice in Spanish recipes. Basmati rice with its fragrant delicate grains is ideal with Indian food, whilst the slightly sticky Thai jasmine rice makes a perfect partner for the clean, fresh flavours of that country's dishes. I keep all of them to hand and they add a very welcome diversity to my cooking.

MUSHROOM RICE WITH COCONUT

Time to make: about 5 minutes
Time to cook: about 25 minutes

Serves 2

185 g (6 oz) Thai jasmine rice

1 stick lemon grass

½ to 1 fresh red chilli

185 g (6 oz) oyster mushrooms

60 g (2 oz) shiitake mushrooms

1 tablespoon sunflower oil

1 bay leaf

250 ml (8 fl oz) coconut milk

salt and freshly ground black
pepper

fresh coriander or basil leaves,
to garnish

Jasmine rice has a wonderful, scented aroma when cooked; in fact, it's so delicious I can eat bowls of it on its own. This dish is subtly flavoured with coconut that doesn't overwhelm the delicate rice. Serve it with Braised Aubergine with Thai Spices on page 54.

1 Rinse the rice in one change of water, then drain. To prepare the vegetables, crush the lemon grass and seed and chop the chilli. Slice the oyster and shiitake mushrooms.
2 Heat the oil in a saucepan with a tight-fitting lid over a medium heat. Add the lemon grass and chilli and cook for 1 minute, stirring. Stir in the mushrooms and bay leaf and stir-fry for 5 minutes until the mushrooms are softened.
3 Stir in the coconut milk and add salt and pepper. Bring to the boil, then lower the heat, cover and cook over a very low heat for 15 to 20 minutes until the rice is tender.
4 Remove the lemon grass and bay leaf, then fluff up the rice with a fork and serve garnished with fresh coriander or basil.

Cook's Tip
If you are cooking Jasmine rice on its own, don't add any salt or pepper as they will mask the delicate flavour of the rice.

CURRIED RICE SALAD WITH MANGO

Time to make: 10 to 15 minutes
Time to cook: 25 minutes

Serves 2

185 g (6 oz) easy-cook Italian brown rice

1 small ripe mango

6 spring onions

2 tablespoons pumpkin seeds

30 g (1 oz) roasted cashew nuts

fresh coriander sprigs and lime wedges, to garnish

Dressing

1 teaspoon mild curry paste

1 lime

3 tablespoons sunflower oil

2 tablespoons chopped fresh coriander

salt and freshly ground black pepper

I lived in the South Pacific for 18 months and had the luxury of a mango tree in my garden. Freshly picked, the fruit has a fragrance and aroma that shop-bought fruit cannot hope to match. The locals used to prepare a wonderful mango or papaya salad with curry spices in the dressing; I've taken the idea for this rice salad, which makes a refreshing light summer meal, particularly if served with warm pitta bread and a minty yogurt raita.

1   Bring a large saucepan of water to the boil over a high heat. Add the rice and simmer for 25 minutes until it is just tender. Drain and rinse under cold water to cool, then drain again. Pat dry with kitchen paper.
2   While the rice is cooking, cut the mango flesh away from the stone, holding it over a bowl to catch any juices, then peel and cut into cubes. Place the cubed flesh into a large bowl.
3   Chop the spring onions, then add them to the bowl along with the pumpkin seeds and cashew nuts.
4   To make the dressing, put the curry paste into a small bowl. Grate in the lime rind and and squeeze in the juice, then whisk in the oil, coriander and salt and pepper.
5   Add the drained rice to the mango mixture, pour over the dressing and toss until completely mixed. Transfer the salad to a serving dish and garnish.

Cook's Tip
Always use a curry paste instead of dry spices when you are making a dressing or recipe that isn't going to be fried. The ingredients in a paste have already been cooked together a little so the flavour is developed and not raw tasting.

Curried Rice Salad with Mango served with a minty yogurt raita.

ROASTED BULGHAR WHEAT WITH A MINTED DRESSING

Time to make: about 25 minutes

Serves 2

125 g (4 oz) bulghar wheat

½ teaspoon cumin seeds

1 bunch spring onions

60 g (2 oz) ready-to-eat dried apricots

30 g (1 oz) dry-roasted cashew nuts

Dressing

5 cm (2 in) piece cucumber

4 tablespoons Greek-style yogurt

1 tablespoon lemon juice

pinch cayenne pepper

1 tablespoon olive oil

1 tablespoon chopped fresh mint

salt and freshly ground black pepper

Bulghar wheat is one of those ingredients that sits at the back of my kitchen cupboard until I suddenly notice it's nearly at its use-by date, then we eat bulghar with everything for a week. It's not that I don't like it, I just don't immediately consider it as an option when thinking up quick meals at the last minute. That changed, however, while I was testing for this book, and this recipe has reminded me of how simple it is to prepare, and how good it is. Also a little of it seems to go a very long way, so it makes an excellent salad for large numbers of people.

Dry roasting bulghar wheat before soaking it gives a lovely nutty flavour to the finished dish.

1   Heat a large, dry frying pan over a high heat until hot, then add the bulghar wheat and cumin seeds and stir until they are golden and toasted. Transfer to a bowl, pour over 625 ml (20 fl oz) boiling water and leave to soak for 20 minutes.
2   Chop the spring onion and the apricots, then set aside.
3   Meanwhile, make the dressing. Grate the cucumber. Place the yogurt in a small bowl and stir until it is smooth. Add the cucumber, lemon juice, cayenne, olive oil and mint and season generously with salt and pepper. Mix until completely combined.
4   Rinse the soaked bulghar under cold water and drain well, squeezing out any excess moisture with your hands. Place in a serving bowl with the spring onions, dried apricots and cashew nuts. Pour over the dressing and toss until well mixed. Serve at once.

Cook's Tip
This roasted bulghar wheat is also good served hot as an accompaniment. Add 1 tablespoon of olive oil and seasoning when you soak the wheat, then transfer it to an ovenproof dish and cover with foil. Bake at 200°C, 400°F, Gas 6 for 15 minutes until piping hot.

QUICK EGG-FRIED RICE

Time to make: 5 minutes
Time to cook: about 20 minutes

Serves 2

6 spring onions

125 g (4 oz) chestnut mushrooms

½ green pepper

185 g (6 oz) Thai jasmine rice, about 315 g (10 oz) cooked weight if you use left-over rice

1 teaspoon sesame oil

2 eggs

2 tablespoons sunflower oil

60 g (2 oz) bean sprouts

60 g (2 oz) frozen peas, thawed

2 tablespoons dark soy sauce

I think this dish is best made with rice cooked the day before as it is drier and the final result is less sticky than if you use freshly cooked rice. I always cook extra rice and store it in the fridge so that I can make fried rice for my children, as it's a real favourite with them. This is my Chinese version – if we've had a pilau rice with curry the night before, I just add extra vegetables and stir in 1 to 2 tablespoons mango chutney and some desiccated coconut to the rice before heating it through to make an Indian version.

1   To prepare the vegetables, chop the spring onions and slice the mushrooms. Core, seed and chop the green pepper half.
2   Bring a large saucepan of water to the boil over a high heat. Add the rice, lower the heat and simmer for 10 minutes until tender. Drain, rinse under cold water to cool and drain again. Pat dry with kitchen paper.
3   Meanwhile, put the sesame oil in a small bowl and beat in the eggs, then set aside.
4   Heat the oil in a wok or deep frying pan over a high heat until almost smoking. Add the spring onions, mushrooms and green pepper and stir-fry for 3 minutes. Add the bean sprouts and peas and continue stir-frying for 1 minute further until the vegetables are piping hot but still crisp.
5   Stir in the rice and stir fry for 3 to 5 minutes until thoroughly heated through. Add the beaten egg and stir gently until set, then stir in the soy sauce until completely mixed. Serve immediately.

Cook's Tip
Cooked rice that has been left at room temperature and not properly reheated can be a cause of food poisoning. So if you make this dish with rice cooked in advance, make sure you transfer the rice to the fridge as soon as it has cooled and don't store it for any longer than 24 hours.

VEGETABLE BIRYANI

Time to make: about 5 minutes
Time to cook: about 25 minutes

Serves 2

1 small onion

1 small carrot

1 small parsnip

60 g (2 oz) green beans

¼ small cauliflower

1 tablespoon sunflower oil

125 g (4 oz) basmati rice

1½ tablespoons biryani paste

100 g (3½ oz) canned chopped tomatoes

375 ml (12 fl oz) vegetable stock

salt and freshly ground black pepper

toasted flaked almonds, raisins and fresh coriander, to garnish

This rice dish is an excellent choice if you suddenly have to cook for large numbers of people at the last minute, as you can use any selection of seasonal vegetables that you have to hand. To save time, I use an excellent ready-made curry paste that I buy at the supermarket, which gives a delicious spicy dish that isn't too fiery. As long as I always have some, along with a ready supply of basmati rice, I feel confident that I have the basis of a satisfying meal at any time. I serve this with a yogurt raita and a selection of chutneys.

1 To prepare the vegetables, finely chop the onion, peel and cut the carrot and parsnip into chunks, halve the green beans and break the cauliflower into florets.
2 Heat the oil in a large flameproof casserole over a medium heat. Add the onion, carrot and parsnip and cook for 5 minutes, stirring occasionally, until lightly browned. Stir in the cauliflower and beans and continue cooking for 1 minute further.
3 Stir in the biryani paste and rice and cook for 1 minute. Add the tomatoes, stock and salt and pepper. Bring to the boil, cover and cook for 15 to 18 minutes until the stock is absorbed and the rice is tender.
4 Fork through the rice and garnish with almonds, raisins and fresh coriander.

Cook's Tip
Soaking the basmati rice before cooking it produces a lighter, less sticky grain, but it does make a recipe longer than 30 minutes to prepare. If you have the time, however, rinse the rice until the water runs clear, then soak it in 625 ml (20 fl oz) water for about 30 minutes. Drain and use as directed in the recipe.

Vegetable Biryani served with a poppadum.

SWEET AND SOUR ROOT VEGETABLES WITH COUSCOUS

Time to make: 5 minutes
Time to cook: 25 minutes

Serves 2

185 g (6 oz) couscous

1 red onion

1 garlic clove

1 parsnip, about 185 g (6 oz)

1 carrot, about 185 g (6 oz)

125 g (4 oz) swede

2 tablespoons olive oil

¼ teaspoon ground cinnamon

¼ teaspoon ground ginger

½ teaspoon paprika

315 ml (10 fl oz) vegetable stock

1 tablespoon clear honey

1 tablespoon balsamic or red wine vinegar

1½ tablespoons chopped fresh rosemary

salt and freshly ground black pepper

Couscous is often mistakenly referred to as a grain but is, in fact, a pasta made from flour and rolled into characteristic tiny balls. In this country most of the couscous you buy only needs soaking to swell the grains, then it can be steamed or warmed through in a covered pan. I prefer the former method as the couscous can then be heated over the simmering stew that it is to accompany, thus saving on both energy and washing up.

1 Place the couscous in a bowl and sprinkle with 185 ml (6 fl oz) cold water. Leave to stand for 15 minutes, stirring occasionally to break up any lumps.
2 Meanwhile, prepare the vegetables. Slice the onion and crush the garlic. Peel and slice the parsnip and carrot. Peel and cube the swede.
3 While the couscous continues soaking, heat half the oil in a large saucepan over a low heat. Add the onion and garlic and cook for 3 minutes, stirring occasionally, until the onion is softened but not browned. Stir in the cinnamon, ginger and paprika with the vegetables and cook over a high heat for 2 to 3 minutes until just golden.
4 Stir in the stock and salt and pepper. Bring to the boil, then lower the heat, cover and simmer for 15 minutes until the vegetables are just tender.
5 After 10 minutes, place the couscous in a metal sieve or colander, cover with a lid and set over the vegetables to steam.
6 Stir the honey, vinegar and rosemary into the vegetable mixture, replace the couscous and return the pan to the boil for about 5 minutes until the liquid is reduced and syrupy.
7 Stir the remaining olive oil through the couscous, then arrange it in a shallow serving dish. Spoon the vegetables over the top and serve immediately.

GREEN HERB RISOTTO

Time to make: 5 minutes
Time to cook: 25 minutes

Serves 2

1 shallot or small onion

1 garlic clove

1 tablespoon olive oil

185 g (6 oz) arborio rice

750 ml (24 fl oz) vegetable stock, hot

4 tablespoons dry white wine

salt and freshly ground black pepper

To finish

45 g (1½ oz) butter

60 g (2 oz) fresh mixed herbs, such as flat-leaf parsley, basil, chives, tarragon, dill or chervil

3 tablespoons freshly grated Parmesan cheese

Risottos are my idea of the perfect comfort food. Rich, creamy and intensely satisfying both to cook and eat, they brighten up the darkest winter evening for me. I make risottos in all the colours of the rainbow, just by following the basic method and adding a vegetable flavouring. Pumpkin, aubergine and courgette are all favourite ingredients. This aromatic version was inspired by my friend Paul Gayler, chef at the Lanesborough Hotel, in London, who has done so much to bring vegetarian food into the 90s.

1 Finely chop the shallot or onion. Crush the garlic. Heat the oil in a heavy-based saucepan. Add the shallot or onion and garlic and cook for about 3 minutes until softened. Add the rice and stir until each grain is coated in oil.
2 Add a ladleful of stock and the wine and simmer over a medium-low heat until the liquid is absorbed, stirring constantly. Continue adding stock, a few tablespoons at a time, stirring frequently, until all the stock is absorbed and the rice is tender and creamy but still with a slight bite. This should take about 20 minutes.
3 While the rice is cooking, place the butter in a blender or food processor with the herbs and process until well blended together.
4 When the stock is absorbed and the rice is tender, stir in the herb butter and Parmesan cheese. Adjust the seasoning if necessary. Serve immediately.

Eggs and cheese dishes

Many new vegetarians make the mistake of replacing meat
with too many dairy products, thus counteracting
the benefits of what should be healthier eating.
So make these cheese-based recipes an
occasional, rather than a daily, treat.

ARTICHOKE, PIMIENTO AND GREEN BEAN TORTILLA

Time to make: about 5 minutes
Time to cook: about 20 minutes

Serves 2

1 onion

60 g (2 oz) green beans

1 large cooked potato

1 canned pimiento, drained

4 canned artichoke hearts, drained

3 tablespoons olive oil

3 eggs, size 3

salt and freshly ground black pepper

While I was testing the recipes for this book, a friend started supplying us with eggs from his free-range chickens. The colour of the yolks are so intense they add a glorious new dimension to egg dishes, and, of course, the flavour is unbeatable.

This Spanish omelette is delicious with any fresh eggs and makes a wonderful centrepiece for a picnic. I make it when I have leftover cooked potatoes in the fridge. In fact, I frequently cook extra so I can make a tortilla the following day.

1 To prepare the vegetables, slice the onion, top and tail the green beans, peel and dice the potato and cut the pimiento into strips. Quarter the artichoke hearts.
2 Heat 1½ tablespoons of the oil in a frying pan over a medium heat. Add the onion and cook for 3 minutes until softened.
3 Meanwhile, bring a saucepan of water to the boil over a high heat and blanch the beans for 2 minutes, then drain and refresh under cold water and drain again. Pat dry with kitchen paper and cut in half.
4 Add the potato and pimiento to the frying pan and cook for a further 3 minutes, stirring occasionally. Add the artichokes and beans and continue cooking for 3 minutes, stirring occasionally.
5 Pour the vegetable mixture into a colander or sieve and drain for a few minutes to get rid of any excess oil.
6 Place the eggs and seasoning in a bowl and beat well. Add the drained vegetables and mix together thoroughly.
7 Heat the remaining oil in a 20 cm (8 in) frying pan over a medium heat. Add the egg mixture and cook for 4 to 5 minutes until the eggs are set and the base is lightly browned.
8 Place a plate over the pan and carefully turn out the tortilla on to the plate, then slide back into the pan and cook the other side for 3 minutes until lightly browned. Serve the tortilla warm or at room temperature, cut into wedges.

Sliding Artichoke, Pimiento and Green Bean Tortilla on to a plate for serving.

SPRING ONION AND CHICK-PEA OMELETTE

Time to make: about 3 minutes
Time to cook: 10 to 15 minutes

Serves 1

4 spring onions

½ garlic clove

½ tomato

1 tablespoon olive oil

90 g (3 oz) canned chick-peas, drained and rinsed

3 eggs

pinch of turmeric

1 tablespoon chopped fresh flat-leaf parsley

salt and freshly ground black pepper

An omelette is one of those dishes that has to be just right for the person who's going to eat it – some like them runny in the centre (me), others prefer a firm set. Ideally a good omelette should combine the two with a golden exterior concealing a moist flavoursome inside. An indifferent omelette, however, used to be the fate of many a vegetarian when eating out, but things are slowly improving. I think it's well worth re-discovering the joys of a properly cooked version in your own home. Chick-peas add a welcome texture to this version. I particularly enjoy this with a simple tomato and onion salad.

1   To prepare the vegetables, chop the spring onions and garlic. Seed and chop the tomato half.
2   Heat half the oil in a frying pan over a medium heat. Add the spring onions, garlic and chick-peas and cook for 3 minutes, stirring occasionally, until the spring onions are wilted. Remove from the pan and keep warm.
3   Place the eggs in a bowl with the turmeric, tomato, parsley and salt and pepper. Beat together well, then stir in the chick-peas and spring onions.
4   Heat the remaining oil in the cleaned pan over a medium heat. When it is hot, add the egg mixture and cook, stirring gently with a fork, until the base begins to set. Stop stirring and continue cooking until the base is golden.
5   Spoon the chick-pea mixture into the centre, fold over the omelette and serve.

FRIED POTATO CAKE WITH EGGS

Time to make: about 5 minutes
Time to cook: 20 to 25 minutes

Serves 2 to 3

500 g (1 lb) waxy potatoes, such as Desirée, thinly sliced

1 onion

2 garlic cloves

6 tablespoons olive oil

4 tablespoons chopped fresh flat-leaf parsley

2 to 4 eggs

salt and freshly ground black pepper

When my husband and I are travelling through south-west France we really look forward to the wonderful local, crisp fried potato dish that makes a perfect accompaniment to fried eggs. There the cooks use goose fat but I've found the dish works almost as well with olive oil. This is not a recipe for anyone watching fat levels, but as an occasional treat for brunch or supper, it's hard to beat. By using olive oil you will be reducing the saturated fat content in any case, and if you serve a green vegetable such as fine beans, and follow with fruit your meal will be good for you, as well as tasting delicious.

1   To prepare the vegetables, thinly slice the potatoes and onions and chop the garlic.
2   Heat the oil in a large deep frying pan over a medium to high heat until almost smoking. Add the potato and onion slices in batches, stirring to coat each batch in oil and seasoning well. Cook, carefully lifting and turning the potatoes with a fish slice, for about 15 minutes until the potatoes are tender and just golden. Try not to let the potatoes break up too much – this will be a real problem if you use a potato with a floury flesh.
3   Add the garlic and parsley to the pan and stir gently to mix them in. Flatten the potatoes into a cake and continue cooking until the base is golden and crisp. Cut the cake into wedges in the pan, remove with a slice and keep warm.
4   Fry the eggs in the oil remaining in the pan, adding them at the end of cooking if desired. Arrange them on top of the potato cake and serve.

MUFFINS WITH GOATS' CHEESE AND TARRAGON EGGS

Time to make: about 5 minutes
Time to cook: about 5 minutes

Serves 1 or 2

1 English muffin

1 teaspoon black olive or sun-dried tomato paste

2 eggs

1 tablespoon milk

1 tablespoon chopped fresh tarragon

small knob of butter

30 g (1 oz) goats' cheese

salt and freshly ground black pepper

fresh tarragon sprigs, to garnish

Mark and I spent the first night of our honeymoon in a beautiful country house hotel (now sadly closed) in deepest Kent. One of the best things about the stay was the wonderful breakfast served outside under one of those huge canvas umbrellas that are now everywhere. At that time I hadn't seen such a thing before and was instantly determined to have one. Be that as it may (we still don't have a smart umbrella eight years on, though I do go to gardening shows and fantasise), the breakfast was delicious; scrambled eggs cooked with fresh tarragon, melt-in-the-mouth croissants and home-made apricot jam, and perfect coffee.

Tarragon is the ideal herb for eggs, so with that dish as inspiration I came up with this. It makes a great snack or light supper for one, or a simple starter for a dinner for two.

1 Split the muffin in half and toast on both sides. Spread the cut sides with the olive or tomato paste.
2 Put the eggs in a small bowl and beat in the milk, tarragon and salt and pepper.
3 Melt the butter in a small non-stick pan over a medium heat. Add the egg mixture and cook, stirring occasionally, until the eggs begin to set but are still creamy.
4 Crumble in the cheese and and stir it in until well mixed. Spoon the egg mixture over the muffins.
5 Serve immediately, garnished with a sprig of fresh tarragon.

Cook's Tip
For fish eaters, a little diced smoked salmon is wonderful added to the egg mixture.

Muffins with Goats' Cheese and Tarragon Eggs

CELERIAC AND STILTON SOUFFLÉS

Time to make: about 15 minutes
Time to cook: 12 to 15 minutes

Serves 2

225 g (8 oz) celeriac

30 g (1 oz) butter

30 g (1 oz) plain flour

155 ml (5 fl oz) semi-skimmed milk

125 g (4 oz) Stilton cheese

4 eggs, separated

1 teaspoon Dijon mustard

pinch of cayenne pepper

salt and freshly ground black pepper

1 tablespoon freshly grated Parmesan cheese, for dusting

Celeriac is a root vegetable with a strong yet subtle flavour of celery. It makes a tasty partner to Stilton, here used together in a soufflé to excellent effect. Soufflés have a reputation for being difficult to make but if you follow the steps carefully and don't open the oven door to check while it is cooking, you shouldn't go wrong.

1   Preheat the oven to 220°C, 425°F, Gas 7. Butter two 10 cm (4 in) soufflé dishes. Peel and finely dice the celeriac.
2   Bring a saucepan of water to the boil over a high heat. Add the celeriac and cook for 10 minutes until tender. Drain well, then purée in a vegetable mouli or a food processor.
3   Meanwhile, melt the butter in a large saucepan over a medium heat. Stir in the flour and cook, stirring constantly, for 1 minute. Off the heat, gradually whisk in the milk, then return the pan to the heat. Bring to the boil, stirring constantly, to give a thick, smooth sauce.
4   Remove the pan from the heat and stir in the celeriac purée and crumble in the Stilton, followed by the egg yolks, mustard and seasoning. Beat together well.
5   Put the egg whites in a clean, dry bowl and whisk until stiff but not dry, then carefully fold them into the cheese and celeriac base.
6   Spoon the soufflé mixture into the prepared dishes and sprinkle with Parmesan cheese. Bake for 12 to 15 minutes until well risen and golden. Serve immediately.

Cook's Tip
This mixture will also make 1 large soufflé or fill 6 small ramekins; always remember to season any egg dish thoroughly to bring out the full flavour.

BAKED EGGS WITH ASPARAGUS AND GREEN BEANS

Time to make: about 3 minutes
Time to cook: about 15 minutes

Serves 1

60 g (2 oz) fresh asparagus tips

60 g (2 oz) fine green beans

small knob of butter

2 tablespoons dry white wine

1 egg, size 1

2 tablespoons crème fraîche

1 tablespoon chopped fresh
tarragon or chives

1 tablespoon freshly grated
Parmesan cheese

salt and freshly ground black
pepper

If I really want to treat myself on one of the rare evenings I get completely to myself, this is the dish I prepare. It is so simple, yet the combination of flavours and texture is so satisfying I am hard pressed to come up with a better recipe. A glass of dry white wine, some good bread to mop up the juices and a good book – what more could you ask for? Asparagus tips are available now most of the year round but as you may have realised, I like cooking with seasonal British produce so ideally I would have to have my solitary evening sometime in May, during asparagus season.

1 Preheat the oven to 180°C, 350°F, Gas 4. To prepare the vegetables, cut the asparagus and beans into 2.5 cm (1 in) lengths on the diagonal.
2 Melt the butter in a small saucepan over a medium heat until foaming. Add the vegetables and cook, stirring, for 1 minute, then add the wine and simmer for a further 2 minutes until the asparagus and beans are almost tender. Add salt and pepper, then arrange over the base of an individual gratin dish.
3 Break the egg over the top of the vegetables and spoon over the crème fraîche. Sprinkle with tarragon, Parmesan cheese and a little salt and pepper.
4 Bake for 12 minutes until the egg is just set. Serve immediately.

Cook's Tip
Sugar snap peas or fresh podded peas work well with the asparagus in this recipe.

EGG AND CAULIFLOWER CURRY

Time to make: about 10 minutes
Time to cook: about 20 minutes

Serves 2

4 eggs

½ small onion

1 garlic clove

250 g (8 oz) cauliflower

1 cm (½ in) piece fresh root ginger

1 tablespoon sunflower oil

1 tablespoon medium curry paste

salt

1 teaspoon tomato purée

1 tablespoon lemon juice

155 ml (5 fl oz) vegetable stock

4 tablespoons plain yogurt

3 tablespoons chopped fresh coriander

I must admit that cauliflower as a vegetable served on its own is not a favourite of mine, as I find it somewhat dull. Add a creamy, well-flavoured sauce, however, and the vegetable is transformed. Cauliflower cheese is a great speedy supper, and in this recipe the vegetable's distinctive texture and subtle flavour is enhanced by a lightly spiced sauce.

A year or two ago I would have rejected out of hand the idea of using a bought curry paste, but with the huge improvement in quality of those available, I now keep a jar handy for when I'm in a hurry or away from my spice cupboard – I tested this recipe while on a self-catering family holiday in Yorkshire when I certainly didn't want to have to buy a whole load of new spices. All this needs in the way of accompaniments are plain boiled rice and a green vegetable.

1   Place the eggs in a small saucepan, cover with cold water and bring to the boil over a high heat. Lower the heat and simmer for 8 minutes, then run them under cold water until they are cool. Shell the eggs and cut them in half, then set aside while you prepare the sauce.
2   Meanwhile, to prepare the vegetables, chop the onion and crush the garlic. Break the cauliflower into florets. Peel and grate the ginger.
3   Heat the oil in a saucepan over a medium heat. Add the onion and cook for 5 minutes, stirring occasionally, until golden. Stir in the garlic, ginger and curry paste and stir-fry for 1 minute, then stir in the tomato purée, lemon juice, salt and vegetable stock.
4   Bring the mixture to the boil, then add the cauliflower florets, lower the heat, cover and simmer for 8 to 10 minutes until the cauliflower is just tender.
5   Stir in the yogurt, 1 tablespoon at a time, then add the coriander. Add the eggs to the sauce, cut sides down, and heat through gently, taking care not to let the sauce boil.

Egg and Cauliflower Curry

CAMEMBERT AND CRANBERRY PARCELS

Time to make: 5 minutes
Time to cook: 15 to 20 minutes

Serves 2

185 g (6 oz) Camembert or Brie cheese

30 g (1 oz) butter

4 sheets phyllo pastry, each about 20 x 30 cm (8 x 12 in)

2 tablespoons cranberry sauce

There was a time when French soft cheese seemed to appear everywhere, either *en croûte* or deep fried, usually accompanied with a dollop of gooseberry jam. I thought the fashion had all but disappeared but then I spotted a rendition on a wine bar menu recently and remembered quite how delicious the combination of melted, gooey cheese and crisp coating could be. I make this with ready-made phyllo pastry but puff pastry works just as well. Serve with a salad of bitter leaves, such as radicchio or frisée, with a sharp dressing.

1 Preheat the oven to 220°C, 425°F, Gas 7. Cut the cheese into 4 wedges.
2 Melt the butter. Brush each sheet of phyllo pastry with melted butter, then fold it in half. Place a piece of cheese in the centre of each sheet of phyllo pastry and top with a dollop of cranberry sauce. Either wrap the pastry round to make a neat parcel or bring the edges together to form a bundle.
3 Dampen a baking sheet with cold water and place the phyllo parcels on it and brush them with the remaining melted butter. Bake for 15 to 20 minutes until the pastry is crisp and golden. Serve immediately.

FRIED MOZZARELLA AND PESTO SANDWICHES

Time to make: 10 minutes
Time to cook: 8 minutes

Serves 2

150 g (5 oz) mozzarella cheese, preferably buffalo

4 thick slices sun-dried tomato bread or black olive bread

2 teaspoons prepared pesto sauce

1 egg

2 to 3 tablespoons olive oil

salt and freshly ground black pepper

With the ever-increasing availability of interesting speciality breads, sandwiches have taken a big step away from endless cheese and pickle or egg and cress. Actually, I am a fan of both of the latter but enjoy the variety of so many of the once-rare, but now widely-available, ingredients. Fried mozzarella sandwiches are a favourite with my family for Sunday night in front of the telly. Served with a big green salad and a glass of red wine for a light supper, they make an impeccable end to the weekend.

1   Cut the mozzarella into thin slices. Remove the crusts from the bread slices.
2   Spread the pesto sauce on 2 slices of bread, then top with the mozzarella cheese slices and season to taste. Make 2 sandwiches and press firmly together.
3   Crack the egg into a shallow dish and beat it with a little salt. Carefully dip the sandwiches into the beaten egg, turning them to coat on both sides.
4   Heat the oil in a large frying pan. Add the sandwiches and cook over a medium heat for 3 to 4 minutes on each side; cook the sandwiches one at a time if your frying pan isn't large enough. Drain the sandwiches on kitchen paper, cut into triangles and serve immediately.

Cook's Tip
Ring the changes with this recipe by using different breads and cheeses. Try Stilton cheese with walnut bread, Brie with olive bread and even Cheddar cheese with raisin bread.

Desserts

Some people express surprise that a book on vegetarian cookery should include sweet recipes, which by definition are free of meat products. Still, I don't see why vegetarians should have to buy a separate book for desserts. Admittedly, I rarely make a dessert mid-week unless we have a guest – we usually have fruit with Greek-style yogurt – but these are the recipes I use when I feel like having a treat.

RED FRUIT FLAMBÉE

Time to make: about 5 minutes
Time to cook: 10 to 15 minutes

Serves 2

125 g (4 oz) fresh strawberries

60 g (2 oz) plums

30 g (1 oz) redcurrants

1 orange

125 g (4 oz) fresh raspberries

60 g (2 oz) golden granulated sugar

2 tablespoons brandy or rum

vanilla ice cream, to serve

When at its best, fresh soft summer fruit needs little enhancement but, if I have some that is a little past its peak, this quick pud uses it to advantage. If you are worried about setting fire to the kitchen or singeing your eyebrows, omit the flambéing and simmer the fruit for one minute after adding the brandy to get rid of the alcohol.

1   To prepare the fruits, halve the strawberries, halve and stone the plums, then thinly slice, and remove all the redcurrants from their strings. Finely grate the orange rind and squeeze the juice.
2   Put the strawberries, plums, redcurrants, orange rind and raspberries in a bowl and mix together.
3   Put the sugar in a heavy-based shallow pan or frying pan over a high heat and heat until it melts and starts to caramelise and go brown. Don't stir it as it melts as it will form into sticky lumps – just move the pan around on the heat to get the heat to the right areas. This will take about 3 minutes.
4   Stir in the orange juice – watch out as the sugar will splutter, then lower the heat and continue stirring until the mixture is syrupy.
5   Add the fruit to the pan and stir over a medium heat for 3 to 4 minutes until heated through. Add the brandy to the pan and set alight with a match. Shake the pan until the flames die down, then serve at once with vanilla ice cream.

Cook's Tip
Turn this into an autumn dish by using apples and blackberries in place of the red fruit. Cook the apple slices first in a knob of butter until they start turning golden, then add them to the syrup with the blackberries and flame as above.

Bubbling Red Fruit Flambée ready for serving.

BANANA BRÛLÉE

Time to make: 5 minutes, plus
  chilling
Time to grill: about 5 minutes

Serves 2

2 large ripe bananas

1 teaspoon lemon juice

1 tablespoon whisky

125 ml (4 fl oz) crème fraîche

**3 tablespoons light muscovado
sugar**

¼ teaspoon ground cinnamon

Fruit brûlées are deservedly popular for quick puddings as they take little preparation and can be made with whatever fruit and topping you have to hand. A dash of booze makes all the difference and turns a family pud into a treat. I use whisky as it tends to be the only spirit we regularly keep in the house and it does go well with fruit but you can also use rum or brandy. This recipe is made with bananas and crème fraîche but feel free to use other toppings – whipped cream, thick yogurt or mascarpone cheese mixed with equal amounts of cream will all be successful.

1 Slice the bananas, then arrange them over the base of a shallow flameproof serving dish. Sprinkle with the lemon juice and whisky.
2 Put the crème fraîche in a bowl and stir until it is smooth, then spread it over the bananas so they are completely covered. Cover the dish and chill until just before serving.
3 Preheat the grill. Mix the sugar and cinnamon together, then sprinkle over the top of the crème fraîche to cover it completely.
4 Put the dish under the grill until the sugar melts and bubbles. Serve immediately.

Cook's Tip
Using different sugars for the topping will give different effects and tastes. Demerara sugar, for example, produces a crunchy topping, while caster sugar melts more evenly into a clear caramel finish. I prefer the taste of muscovado sugar with bananas but do experiment to find your own favourite.

APRICOT AND LEMON PUDDINGS

Time to make: about 8 minutes
Time to bake: 12 to 15 minutes

Serves 2

85 g (3 oz) self-raising flour, plus extra for flouring the work surface

30 g (1 oz) butter, well chilled, plus extra for buttering the ramekins

1 tablespoon caster sugar

30 g (1 oz) rice flour

1 teaspoon grated lemon rind

2 to 3 tablespoons semi-skimmed milk, plus a little extra for glazing

1 tablespoon flaked almonds

clotted cream, to serve, optional

Filling

220 g (7 oz) can apricots in natural juice

1 tablespoon demerara sugar

When I was a child, my family and I used to visit a favourite restaurant in a Tudor farmhouse in Kent. It served the most wonderful traditional English food, the type now served in smart restaurants across the country. I remember that the puds were particularly good, especially the apricot pie. It was intensely fruity with a crust that was more like a scone than pastry. This is my quick homage to that pie.

1   Preheat the oven to 200°C, 400°F, Gas 6. Butter 2 large ramekins.
2   Sift the flour into a mixing bowl. Dice the butter, then rub it into the flour with your fingertips until the mixture resembles fine breadcrumbs.
3   Stir in the sugar, ground rice and lemon rind, then add enough milk to make a soft dough.
4   Turn out the dough on to a lightly floured work surface and roll out until it is about 2 cm (¾ in) thick. Use a fluted biscuit cutter to cut out two 9 cm (3½ in) rounds.
5   Divide the apricots and their juice between the ramekins. Sprinkle with sugar.
6   Top each pudding with a dough round and brush with a little milk, then scatter with almonds.
7   Bake the puddings for 12 to 15 minutes until the topping is well risen and golden. Serve with clotted cream, if you like.

Cook's Tip
You can use any canned fruit for this dessert but be sure not to use any fruit in a syrup, as the end result will be too sweet.

INSTANT BLACKCURRANT AND RASPBERRY SORBET

Time to make: about 20 minutes,
plus up to 1 hour freezing

Serves 2

125 g (4 oz) frozen blackcurrants

125 g (4 oz) frozen raspberries

45 g (1½ oz) caster sugar

1 tablespoon kirsch (optional)

1 egg white, size 3

mint sprigs, to garnish

Amaretti biscuits or sponge fingers, to serve

This method of making an instant sorbet was shown to me by Prue Leith when I was a student at her cookery school in London. I have been making variations on the theme ever since, and as a recipe its adaptability and ease of preparation made it an obvious choice for this book.

Make this just before you sit down to eat and return it to the freezer while eating your main course; it will be soft and scoopable when you need to serve it!

1   Remove the currants and raspberries from the freezer and leave them to stand at room temperature for 15 minutes to soften slightly.
2   Put the blackcurrants and raspberries in a blender or food processor, add the sugar and kirsch, if using, and process until smooth but still icy.
3   Put the egg white in a bowl and whisk until stiff, then fold it into the fruit purée with a large metal spoon.
4   Transfer the mixture to a rigid container and freeze for up to 1 hour until firm. Serve in scoops, garnish with mint sprigs. Accompany with sweet biscuits.

Cook's Tip
Eat this sorbet within a day or two of making as it will deteriorate in quality as the fruit has been frozen twice. For a firmer set, make the sorbet without the alcohol as it inhibits the freezing process.

Instant Blackcurrant and Raspberry Sorbet

HOT MOCHA SOUFFLÉS

Time to make: about 10 minutes
Time to cook: 12 to 15 minutes

Serves 2

---
1 tablespoon caster sugar
---
30 g (1 oz) dark chocolate
---
2 tablespoons crème fraîche

¼ teaspoon instant coffee granules
---
2 eggs, separated

½ tablespoon brandy or rum
---
icing sugar, for dusting

A hot chocolate soufflé is my emergency stand-by if we have unexpected guests – it's quick and simple to prepare, I've usually got all the ingredients and everybody loves it. This recipe doesn't involve making a sauce; it's based on chocolate melted with cream which gives an intense flavour. I like really bitter chocolate, so I suggest you use a dark chocolate with a high percentage of cocoa solids and throw in a little coffee and brandy for added kick. Prepare the base before the meal, then whisk up the egg whites and fold them in as soon as you finish eating. The soufflés take about 15 minutes to cook but no one seems to mind waiting!

1   Preheat the oven to 200°C, 400°F, Gas 6. Butter 2 ramekins and dust with half the caster sugar. Finely chop the chocolate.
2   Place the chocolate, crème fraîche and coffee together in a small saucepan over a low heat and heat gently, stirring, until the chocolate melts. Remove the pan from the heat.
3   Stir the egg yolks and brandy into the chocolate mixture until well mixed.
4   Put the egg whites in a bowl and whisk until stiff but not dry, then whisk in the sugar. Lightly fold the egg whites into the chocolate mixture.
5   Divide the soufflé mixture between the prepared ramekins and place them in a roasting tin half filled with hot water. Bake for 12 to 15 minutes until puffed up, dust with icing sugar and serve immediately.

Cook's Tip
To get the lightest results, make sure the eggs are at room temperature and the bowl is completely clean before whisking the egg whites.

FRESH RASPBERRY CRISP

Time to make: 10 minutes, plus
  cooling
Time to cook: 20 minutes

Serves 2

60 g (1 oz) rolled oats

30 g (1 oz) demerara sugar

15 g (½ oz) slivered almonds

1 teaspoon sesame seeds

1½ tablespoons clear honey

75 ml (2½ fl oz) Greek-style
yogurt

2 tablespoons mascarpone
cheese

185 g (6 oz) fresh raspberries

raspberries and mint leaves, to
decorate

I make up a quantity of this oat mixture and serve it with yogurt and fruit for breakfast or sprinkled over fresh fruit and baked like a crumble. It is a bit of a push to get the oat mixture roasted and cooled within the thirty-minute limit but it's so simple that I've included it anyway, as the oats can continue cooling while you enjoy your main course, and the dessert assembled at the last minute. If you do make up the oat mixture in advance, it will keep for up to one month in an air-tight container.

1   Preheat the oven to 160°C, 325°F, Gas 3. Put the oats, sugar, almonds, sesame seeds and honey in a bowl and mix together.
2   Place the mixture in a small roasting tin and bake for 20 minutes, stirring occasionally, until the mixture is crisp and golden. Spread out on a plate or tray and leave to cool.
3   Just before serving, stir the yogurt and mascarpone cheese together. Arrange a few raspberries in the base of 2 tall glasses, sprinkle with a layer of the oat mixture and spoon over some of the yogurt mixture.
4   Continue layering up, finishing with the yogurt mixture. Decorate with raspberries and mint and serve.

Cook's Tip
If raspberries aren't available, I sometimes use peaches and ginger biscuits in the same way. Peel and dice a couple of ripe peaches, crush 4 ginger biscuits and layer up with crème fraîche.

BAKED AMARETTI PEACHES

Time to make: about 5 minutes
Time to cook: 15 to 20 minutes

Serves 2

2 large ripe peaches

4 Amaretti biscuits or large macaroons

1 egg yolk

2 tablespoons brandy, orange liqueur or orange juice

ice cream or Greek-style yogurt, to serve

Amaretti biscuits are those little almond biscuits in multi-coloured papers which, it seemed, were always served at the end of meals in Italian restaurants when I was a child. My sisters and I always looked out for them, not because of the biscuits inside but for the papers themselves. They were transformed by some magic of my mother's into little cones which she then set alight, and we would watch open-mouthed as they floated up to the ceiling, burning brightly. The friendly Italian proprietor must have viewed our arrival in his premises with trepidation as he ran to check his fire cover! Anyway, the biscuits make a quick flavouring for baked peaches; serve with premium-quality vanilla ice cream for a real treat.

1   Preheat the oven to 180°C, 350°F, Gas 4. Halve the peaches, twist to separate the halves and carefully remove the stones. Lightly crush the biscuits.
2   Place the halved peaches on a baking sheet.
3   Put the crushed biscuits in a bowl with the egg yolk and mix together.
4   Spoon the mixture into the cavity in the peach halves left by the stones. Sprinkle with the liqueur or orange juice.
5   Bake for 15 to 20 minutes until the peaches are just tender. Serve warm with ice cream or Greek-style yogurt.

Cook's Tip
Amaretti biscuits are available in Italian delicatessens or supermarkets.

PEAR BATTER PUDDING

Time to make: 10 minutes
Time to cook: 15 to 20 minutes

Serves 2

2 small, ripe pears

1 egg, size 1

6 tablespoons single cream

1 tablespoon caster sugar

1 tablespoon ground almonds

1 tablespoon rum

pinch of ground cinnamon

large knob of butter

icing sugar, to dust

I've been experimenting recently with different ways to use the basic Yorkshire pudding batter, and this is one of the results. It is a cross between a French clafoutis and a Yorkshire pudding but the end result is far richer than either, and I think it makes a splendid end to any meal. Cook this in a simple, shallow gratin dish, dust with icing sugar and you have a pud fit for a king.

1 Preheat the oven to 200°C, 400°F, Gas 6. Peel, core and slice the pears.
2 Arrange the pears in the base of a small, shallow ovenproof dish.
3 Put the egg, cream, sugar, ground almonds, rum and cinnamon in a bowl and beat together. Melt the butter and stir it into the batter.
4 Pour the batter over the pear slices. Bake for 15 to 20 minutes until puffy and golden. Dust with icing sugar and serve immediately.

USEFUL ADDRESSES FOR MAIL ORDER

Steamboat Oriental Foods,
PO. Box 452, Bradford
West Yorkshire BD4 7TF.
Telephone: 01274 742936.
For an extensive range of oriental
foods and cooking accessories.

Freshlands Wholefoods
(Used to be known as Clearspring)
196 Old Street, London EC1V 9FR.
Telephone: 0171 250-1708.
For a wide range of organic and
macrobiotic wholefoods.

The Fresh Food Company,
341A Ladbroke Grove,
London W10 6HA.
Telephone: 0181 969-0351.
Fresh food boxes of organic fruit and
vegetables, and all the pastes and oils
used in this book.

INDEX